Surrounded by Smarter
Lessons I Learned the Hard Way

Dedicated to my loving wife, Maryellen, my children, Nicole and Chris, my parents, family and friends. Also, to the hundreds of wonderful people whom which I have had the pleasure to associate with over my career, I thank you all for encouraging me, teaching me and supporting me all these years.

All rights reserved. No part of this book may be reproduced or modified in any form, including photocopying, recording, or by any information storage and retrieval system, without permission in writing from the author. May 10, 2019

ISBN: 9781097773954

Contents

SURROUNDED BY SMARTER   1
   Dedicated   1

CONTENTS   2

PREFACE   1

PREREQUISITE   4
Work Ethic   4

SECTION 1- PROPOSITION   6

MODULE 1- COMMITMENT   7
Lesson 1-1- Passion   7

MODULE 1- COMMITMENT   8
Lesson 1-2- "I already tried that and it did not work"   8

MODULE 1- COMMITMENT   10
Lesson 1-3- Stubborn Perseverance   10

MODULE 1- COMMITMENT   11
Lesson 1-4- Your Career is not a straight line up   11

MODULE 2- VISION   13
Lesson 2-1- See it as you want it   13

MODULE 2- VISION   14
Lesson 2-2- Make sure it is yours   14

MODULE 2- VISION 15
Lesson 2-3- Value Proposition 15

MODULE 3- PLANNING AND MODELING 16
Lesson 3-1- Underneath It All- the Numbers 16

MODULE 3- PLANNING AND MODELING 18
Lesson 3-2- Conservative approach to forecasting and budgeting 18

MODULE 3- PLANNING AND MODELING 20
Lesson 3-3- Startup Finances 20

MODULE 4- BUSINESS ETHICS 22

MODULE 5- BUSINESS PHILOSOPHY 24
Lesson 5-1- Manage with a long-term view, but… 24

MODULE 5 - BUSINESS PHILOSOPHY 26
Lesson 5-2- Reputation is everything 26

MODULE 5- BUSINESS PHILOSOPHY 28
Lesson 5-3- What I Learned from my Mentors 28
- Cliff 28
- George 28
- Hank 28
- Charlie 28
- Dave 28

MODULE 5- BUSINESS PHILOSOPHY 33
Lesson 5-4- Making Career Decisions 33

MODULE 5- BUSINESS PHILOSOPHY 35
Lesson 5-5 - Decision Making- Not a democratic process 35

SECTION 2- PROCESS	36
MODULE 6- RECRUITING AND HIRING	**37**
Lesson 6-1- Surround Yourself with Smart Hard-Working People- Then try to Keep Up!	37
MODULE 6- RECRUITING AND HIRING	**40**
Lesson 6-2- Job Match is Paramount	40
MODULE 6- RECRUITING AND HIRING	**42**
Lesson 6-3- Make sure Managers can Manage	42
MODULE 6- RECRUITING AND HIRING	**45**
Lesson 6-4- Role of a Sales Manager or Business Owner	45
MODULE 6- RECRUITING AND HIRING	**48**
Lesson 6-5- The Rule of Three	48
MODULE 6- RECRUITING AND HIRING	**50**
Lesson 6-6- Due Diligence	50
MODULE 6- RECRUITING AND HIRING	**52**
Lesson 6-7- The Cost of Making a Bad Hire	52
MODULE 6- RECRUITING AND HIRING	**53**
Lesson 6-8- Beware of Rainmakers	53
MODULE 6- RECRUITING AND HIRING	**55**
Lesson 6-9- College recruits, the pros and cons	55
MODULE 7- CUSTOMER FOCUSED BUSINESS	**57**
Lesson 7-1- The customer is not always right, but always important	57

MODULE 7- CUSTOMER FOCUSED BUSINESS	58
Lesson 7-2- Another Loan	58
MODULE 7- CUSTOMER FOCUSED BUSINESS	60
Lesson 7-3- Managing customer expectations	60
MODULE 7- CUSTOMER FOCUSED BUSINESS	62
Lesson 7-4- Live in their shoes	62
MODULE 7- CUSTOMER FOCUSED BUSINESS	64
Lesson 7-5- Handling Irate Customers.	64
MODULE 7- CUSTOMER FOCUSED BUSINESS	65
Lesson 7-6- Fulfill their needs and you do not have to sell	65
MODULE 7- CUSTOMER FOCUSED BUSINESS	67
Lesson 7-7- Addition by Subtraction	67
MODULE 8- PEOPLE MANAGEMENT	69
Lesson 8-1- What motivates people	69
MODULE 8- PEOPLE MANAGEMENT	73
Lesson 8-2- Managing Up	73
MODULE 8- PEOPLE MANAGEMENT	75
Lesson 8-3- Manage everyone the same and you lose	75
MODULE 8- PEOPLE MANAGEMENT	76
Lesson 8-4- Separation Interview should not last more than five minutes	76
MODULE 8- PEOPLE MANAGEMENT	79

Lesson 8-5-Being fired should never be a surprise	79
MODULE 8- PEOPLE MANAGEMENT	**81**
Lesson 8-6- Catch people doing good things but no Participation Certificates	81
MODULE 8- PEOPLE MANAGEMENT	**82**
Lesson 8-7- Never fly at 30,000 feet	82
MODULE 8- PEOPLE MANAGEMENT	**85**
Lesson 8-8- Coaching Sales to create Referrals	85
MODULE 9- WORKING ENVIRONMENT	**87**
Lesson 9-1- Organizational structure must make business sense	87
MODULE 9- WORKING ENVIRONMENT	**90**
Lesson 9-2- Cancer in the Organization	90
MODULE 9- WORKING ENVIRONMENT	**92**
Lesson 9-3- Meetings- useful but not a social hour	92
FINAL THOUGHTS	**94**
RECOMMENDED READING	**96**

Preface

I would like to set the stage for reading this book. For clarity purposes you should know my stated goal.

"I want to create a guide that shares my learning experiences, both those taught formally and those gleaned from the real world, with those either starting out in a business career or those contemplating opening their own business."

Not every lesson is for everyone and every circumstance. Also, in a few places in the book I have included a few sentences of some personal views, reflection and memories. Please bear with me when I venture from the straight lessons and the goal of this book. You may read them if you wish. You may agree or disagree or find them interesting, but I felt it necessary to get these on paper. I have used some personal anecdotes at times to illustrate the point of the Lesson. Lastly, most of my career was spent in the Mortgage banking industry. Thus, some examples reference that fact. I truly believe though that most all of my lessons apply to most businesses.

About the Title…

"Surrounded by Smarter" It was Jack Welch that said, *"I was never the smartest guy in the room. From the first person I hired, I was never the smartest guy in the room. And that's a big deal. And if you're going to be a leader - if you're a leader and you're the smartest guy in the world - in the room, you've got real problems."*

https://www.brainyquote.com/quotes/jack_welch_451369

Smart guy that Jack Welch. Looking back at my business career, I am humbled by the number of hard working, dedicated, and very smart people with whom I surrounded myself. Particularly, some of my biggest successes were a result of others coming up with good ideas. I guess I was rarely the smartest person in the room so I listened to others. I was not always the first to see the next big thing or impending situation. But I always learned from the smarter ones.

About the Subtitle…

"Business lessons I learned the hard way" refers to the fact that I did not begin my adult life doing all the necessary things to prepare myself for my career. Namely, I did not finish college. Frankly it may be nearly impossible to replicate my career in today's world. It was harder to get a job for me without the degree. But today it may be impossible, unless you invent or create something that is unique and needed. I am not saying that I did not have the education to succeed. In my early career I was fortunate to work for an organization that invested heavily in training and I was able to take undergraduate and graduate level classes that provided much needed education for me. I was also blessed with some amazing mentors that taught me what they learned in school and in business. It was the hard way because, not having the education before being married and having children and having to make a living, retarded my access to career jobs early on. But I did have a solid point of reference thanks to my parents. They showed me;

- That hard work never hurt anyone
- Doing the right thing is the right thing to do
- To never forget who you are and never think you are better than anyone else
- To always be humble

Back to the development of this book. I am not a trained writer. I am also not one to be overly verbose in my written communications. My favorite class in college and the only English class I ever liked was called "Technical Report Writing". I do not remember the professor's name, but when he came into the first class I was immediately impressed. Yes, I am so old that professors actually taught classes in person. His sleeves were rolled up and he said that we would not be writing in flowery prose. We would state the situation, write what we saw, what we thought and what we would do. That's it, no theatrics. That fit and still fits my mentality. I was always praised for my written communications and according to many, I provided clear crisp information and direction. Therefore, as I was writing this book, it struck me that the sections I was calling chapters were in reality thoughts or observations that often were only one or two pages. After writing all of the sections of the book in its first draft, I thought about going back and writing much more in each section thus flowering up and increasing the size of the section to look much more like a chapter. I started with the first lesson and after several hours and many days I realized that this was not me and it was a chore to do and I was not adding to the amount of learning. So, I stopped. I did go back and add things I later thought would mean something to the sections, but that was it. Then I was faced with deciding what to call these sections. They did not seem large enough to be called chapters. I decided to call them Lessons.

I had an introspective moment. I do not have many. I thought about the question as to why I had to write down these Lessons. What authority or level of intellect gave me the right? I think I had 3 main reasons.

1. Much of what I have shared was not written in any books on business or management. Nobody sat me in a class and taught these things to me. Much of what I have been taught in classes on business actually was intuitive. I somehow knew it but did not see it in a linear way. I feel that I would have liked to have this information much earlier in my career.
2. There are several pieces in this book that discuss ethics and morals. I look at the world we live in and see so much discord and so much compromise to people's beliefs and sense of right and wrong. Doing the right thing, making decisions as if it will be published in the Wall Street Journal and being a decent person and business leader seem to be concepts that are fading from our world. I am here to tell you that the day will come when you will be proud of doing it right and the few extra dollars you could have stolen does not make your life better. I feel these concepts must be preserved
3. I have had the privilege of working with and for some of the best people in the world. The people that have encouraged me, mentored me and performed for me are all close to my heart. Younger people I have worked with have said kind things to me about how much I taught them. This gave me the purpose to try and provide some of my thoughts to others starting into the business world or running their own business.

There you have it. I hope you enjoy this book and I pray that at least one lesson helps you be more successful in your career.

Prerequisite

Work Ethic

I would like to set the tone for this book by sharing the most basic prerequisite to success in business and in life in general. **Work Ethic**

It all comes back to Work Ethic. If I had to hire a person based upon only one quality it would be their work ethic. It is also the easiest way to not only stick out as an employee but it is the quality that best insulates yourself from layoffs, reorganizations and business failure Also, in the context of this book, it will be the top determinant factor as to whether or not you and/or your business succeeds.

In my experience less than 10% of the people we see have a superior work ethic. These are the superstars, smartest, easy to recognize and usually it comes naturally to them. Another 10% have a very good work ethic. These are those over-achievers, steady contributors and hard workers that are the backbone of any organization. That means 20% of the people are at least very good. This supports the old 80/20 truism that says "20% of the people accomplish 80% of the tasks in any company". This rule applies universally whether it is sales activities or making widgets.

Work ethic is best described as the priority you place on your performance. What priority you place on your social life versus your job? If the importance of your job is so far below the importance you place upon your social life that you are just getting the basics done and out the door at 5 PM, take every vacation and sick day each year, you certainly are not in the top 20%. *I am not talking about family; I am speaking of social life. Family is everything. The work/family/social life balance is most difficult and is the subject of many books. It is a delicate balancing act.* However, if you want to take a leadership role in an organization or manage your own business, job performance must be a priority. So, what fuels this work ethic? Obviously, there are certain characteristics that feed them and only the top 20% have these in combination. I believe that the list below captures the minimum characteristics;

- *Sense of non-entitlement*- What do I mean by this? It is an understanding that the world does not owe them anything, and furthermore, will not give them anything. It is a sense that they are responsible for the good things and the bad things that happen to them in business and in life. It means paying their dues and not to expect things to come to them without earning it through hard work and sacrifice. Their life and career will not come instantaneously like a microwave oven. It's more like a slow cooker. It is fine to desire the new car, white picket fence home and a boat, but to expect that you should have them immediately is a recipe for less success and economic disaster. In a nutshell, it is taking personal responsibility for your life.

- *Eagerness to please-* Top performers understand that they must make their customers happy and always do a little more than expected or requested. Who is their Customer? Certainly, people who pay them for the product or service, but their customers are also their boss and their peers that rely upon them to perform. Please these people and success will follow.
- *Thirst for knowledge-* Top performers have a natural curiosity and want to learn how to do and learn how it works. This keeps them interested and makes their work seem more like recreation.
- *Pride in performance-* Finally and lastly these people take pride in being the very best at what they do. Often financial reward is less valued than being recognized and knowing that they make it happen. They often will work harder to win a recognition trip than just to earn more money. Money is important to them of course but not always as strong a motivator. I will have more on motivation later in the book.

In summary, Work Ethic is where it all starts. If you have it, show it and be consistent. If it does not come naturally and you want to excel in business and life, look at your priorities and learn to have this quality. It will serve you well.

Section 1- Proposition

Module 1- Commitment
Lesson 1-1- Passion

I have purposely placed this section called Commitment at the beginning of this book. That is because your commitment to all that you do or the person you are will determine whether or not you have a chance to succeed. In other words, without commitment failure is certain. You will face obstacles, challenges, unforeseen setbacks, betrayals, disillusionment and tragedies in your life and career. During these difficult times, the only thing that will motivate you to fight on is your commitment. While commitment takes many forms and are in many categories, I have highlighted four of them in this Module.

I will begin with a brief but important word on passion.

I know of no truly heroic, successful and or motivating person in history who did not possess a high level of passion. Whether it was a social or moral calling, a cause they deeply believe in, support for their country or the welfare, care or safety of others, these people all had a passion. They have a burning desire to be somebody or do something that really is meaningful even if it is only to themselves. It must be something that you really love to do or be. Sometimes the passion is so consuming that other parts of these people's lives suffered. Some devoted their entire being to their passion to the detriment to their family. I certainly do not condone that. You must be able to balance all that is important in your life and be present for all of them.

Life is hard. Every business has its challenges and things that are not fun, exhilarating or even noble that must be accomplished every day. There is no business or line of work that is easy and fun and profitable. You can find anything that is one of the three. Once in a while you can find something that is two, but never three. So, what makes you want to stick with something for an extended period of time? You must have some level of love for the business, cause or calling's success in order to stick with it through those times. You must be passionate about what you do to give yourself any chance at success. It is important because during those times when you question everything you must have the passion for the mission.

Module 1- Commitment

Lesson 1-2- "I already tried that and it did not work"

Once you find that passion then you can defend your business. Invariably any idea or concept developed by someone will be met with the naysayers stating that it will not work. Sometimes it is someone who says they have tried it and it does not work or there is too much competition to work. How many times did Edison hear that electric cannot create light? How many times did Bill Gates hear that he could not compete with IBM?

This does not mean that you should not seek other's advice and ask for opinions of those you respect. Indeed, such research and thought are a pre-requisite to any decision to proceed with a plan or idea. You should gather your research and convince yourself of the validity or lack thereof of your concept. Then and only then, after building a plan that makes sense to you, should you make the commitment to make a go for it.

Let's examine the two types of comments against your plan/idea:

"I/We've tried it and it did not work"
- What exactly did they try?
- Who were the players?
- How long did they try?
- When did they try?
- Did they try several variations before abandoning the idea?
- Did they have my passion?

These are the questions to consider when weighing this comment from others. Your methodology can be very different than theirs and that variation can make all the difference in the world. For example, Edison's choice of the type of wire used in the light bulb made a success after hundreds of failures.

Did the people involved have the knowledge, commitment and work ethic that you possess? That will make all the difference because it will take those qualities to make anything work.

Finally, timing is everything and if someone tried this in a different economic environment or before the idea fit into the world that existed then, failure then could mean success today.

"You are just too small to take on this project as the big guys will eat you up."

- Competition does not happen on a Global level. It is person to person, company to company. Starting with that, expansion can be nothing more than doing more of the same. As a smaller player a 20% growth in business might be one more customer, so the impact of the one deal is enormous.
- Customer Service and delivery of product has the largest impact upon success. So, focusing on this can help you compete on something other than price.
- Look to the smaller customers in your market. The big guys will often avoid dealing with these people leaving them for you.

Bottom line, once you have convinced yourself, put the blinders on and stay committed.

Module 1- Commitment

Lesson 1-3- Stubborn Perseverance

A realistic approach to any venture involves understanding that it will take several attempts to achieve any level of success. Variations will have to be implemented before any success is achieved. To expect that it will work the first time out will only set you up for disappointment and may cause you to give up. Stubborn perseverance is a requisite to your success. Once you have determined that this is what you want to do and it is feasible, nothing should stand in your way, including failure.

You will, no doubt, need to make some adjustments to your plan or business model. While it may end up being a little different than your original vision, if you are comfortable with the end result, embrace it. Stubbornness to the overall dream should not be confused with a refusal to make some adjustments along the way. Let your gut tell you if it is right. The stomach test is a valuable tool in making decisions and mentioned later in this book.

After each stumble, do not dwell on the disappointment as every one of them brings you closer to the finish line. Do the analysis of what did not work. Was it the people, timing, approach, marketing or something else? Make the necessary adjustments and try it again. The learning experience alone is valuable and makes you better next time.

In summary, decide on a goal, stubbornly persevere and embrace every misstep as a means to an end.

Module 1- Commitment
Lesson 1-4- Your Career is not a straight line up

It is true, that every experience, good or bad, is a learning experience. Adding to your knowledge base and experience continues throughout your life and it makes you more capable and valuable each day. Unfortunately, your career path is not so predictable. I can look back at times when my career lurched forward faster than it should have. There also were periods of time when my career slid sideways or worse, slid back. These are the tough times and you will experience them. So, it is best to analyze them to avoid making irrational decisions that are not best for you in the long run.

It is said that luck is created when preparation and opportunity meet. Advancing your career can only occur when you possess the experience, have the opportunity and you are recognized by the decision makers as a candidate.

There will be times when the opportunity is there, but you are not ready. It is very important that you recognize the fact that you are not ready even if others think you are. Do not confuse this with times when you lack the confidence that you are ready. However, seeking an opportunity when you are truly not ready is not normally a good idea. If you do take the opportunity you will struggle to catch up or worse fail. In business as in life you are only as good as your last review. If you struggle to catch you may not hit goals and be viewed poorly. You may be labeled as having reached your maximum potential or worse a flawed employee. If the opportunity is there and you are truly not ready, I recommend holding off for the next one. Learn and then demonstrate to your superiors that you are ready.

There will be times when you are ready but there is no opportunity. Even if you are recognized as a candidate, if there is no opportunity, it is not going to happen, at least not now. That is where research and exploration into another division or another company is prudent. There may be times when moving to another division or company provides opportunity. You should carefully consider moving to another company. Make sure that it is the kind of place and has the possibility of continued upward mobility. Moving too quickly and too often is not usually good for your career. However, be sure not to be labeled a job-hopper. Put your time in and stay with it as long as you can. Generally, your best opportunities will come at the company for which you are a known entity. But in today's world job hopping for the right reasons is not as damaging as in the past. Just make sure you do your homework before making the move.

There can be a time when the opportunity is there and you are ready, yet the powers that be do not recognize you as a candidate. This is most frustrating and usually is your own fault. You should conduct yourself in a manner consistent with a superior performer. Also show leadership skills and create or volunteer for cutting edge innovations and/or initiatives. Your job is to sell yourself to the decision makers regarding promotions every day by demonstrating the knowledge, work ethic and desire to move up. You should build the reputation that keeps you top of mind to them when the opportunity is there and you are prepared.

Sometimes your career is sent backwards. Layoffs, cutbacks, downsizing or company bankruptcy can eliminate your job. That is when the hard work you do to gain knowledge and be prepared for various roles pays off. You should be well versed in all aspects and levels of work in your company. You will most likely have to reinvent yourself several times in your career. You should certainly carefully consider whether you should do this, but once you do, embrace the reinvention. Remember, that even if it fails, you have added much more experience to your career and resume. Get up dust yourself off, do not feel sorry for yourself and go get another opportunity.

So be prepared for those times when your career is sliding sideways or backwards because they will come. Make sure you have a realistic view of your capabilities and that someone you respect confirms your readiness. Time and repetition are the best ingredients to ready yourself. Your career is not a sprint, but a marathon.

Module 2- Vision

Lesson 2-1- See it as you want it

Most successful athletes share a common trait. They have the ability to visualize the move they will make and the positive results that will result. A professional golfer sees the swing and the putt going into the hole. The Quarterback sees the pass in the receiver's hands.

The most successful leaders in our history also share this trait. Ted Kennedy eulogizing his brother Bobby said, "… some people see things as they are and say why, Bobby saw things as they should be and said why not?"

This is a powerful message. People with a vision are the ones that create in this world. They create businesses, movements and affect the lives of others. When the vision results in a positive change or creation it is usually rewarded by success.

As you look at a new venture, be it a job or a new business, you must be able to visualize and be comfortable with the end result. All too often people have a short-sided vision and do not see far enough and consequently do not know where it might lead or look like in the end. In these cases, people usually suffer from poor planning and often fail.

Only you can create your vision. You must go through the process of developing it. You will benefit from being able to share your vision with others. They can only aid you in your venture if they see and share your vision.

So first think through the vision to the end game. If it is the result you desire, then internalize the vision and make plans with a view of the end game or said in a different way, make it your own. Of course, there are more steps to the process of creating the vision, like making sure the numbers work. But nothing makes sense unless and until you see what you want it to be and then never lose sight of it.

Module 2- Vision

Lesson 2-2- Make sure it is yours

Your level of commitment to your business or career is directly related to your success. Your level of commitment requires a strong belief in your vision of your goal, career or business. So, it stands to reason that the vision must be your vision. Many times, well-meaning people in your life provide advice as to what kind of work or business is best for you. You should encourage others to provide their perspective so you might grow in knowledge. You should use this knowledge to formulate your own opinion and perspective. From this your vision can be developed. Too often however, we listen to these people, especially people that we are close to or those we respect, and begin to change our vision into theirs. While this advice and feedback is valuable, it cannot replace your vision. This is especially true if you are fortunate enough to see your vision as your passion. Taking advice and guidance from others should never cloud what you really want.

You should keep your vision in mind while making any large decisions and many smaller ones. The guidance from deciding through the prism of your own vision is something that will help you maintain your compass settings. Do not waver from your vision to please others. They do not have your set of skills and experiences and cannot be inside your head. Stay steadfast in following your vision as keeping your vision in front of you at all times will pay large dividends.

Following your vision is a journey. Your vision is a living thing and may change over time. As long as the change is your you should stay on course. Over time adjustments to this vision may be warranted. This is perfectly fine as long as it remains your vision. If you discover that your vision is not the right vision for you, begin the process again. Then rediscover your new vision and press on. Learn from the experience and look for your next vision armed with a larger perspective. Just Make sure it is yours!

Module 2- Vision

Lesson 2-3- Value Proposition

The final step in the commitment process is to make sure you understand the value proposition for your idea will be to the customer. Simply put, "What demand, what value and what will your customer be willing to pay for your product or service." This is central to everything that follows. You cannot make any realistic budgeting plans if you do not know these things. It should actually be the first thing you consider when deciding to move on to your endeavor. You can make a wonderful product and come to find nobody wants it. You can make a wonderful product and come to find that nobody values it enough to buy yours. And finally, you may make a wonderful product and find that consumers will not pay enough for it to make a profit.

This is part of the preliminary homework you must do in the very beginning. The way you go about this is different depending on the product or service but a few steps are common. You should see what the competition is making or offering and see the price-points to understand the financials. Researching the internet and looking at competitor's advertisements can be a great start. If there are retail outlets that sell the product or service, visit them and see the price as well as the way they position the product or service to the customer.

Research the internet for chat rooms on the topic. You can gain much insight by seeing what others are saying. You can better understand the value they place on it. Also look for the particular things they value in the product or service. What are their hot buttons? Who are the customers?

The value proposition must be part of your deliberation process before committing to any endeavor. Take your time and ask everyone.

Module 3- Planning and Modeling
Lesson 3-1- Underneath It All- the Numbers

This is one of the few absolutes in business-

"Nothing works unless the Numbers do".
This man sold widgets. He bought them for $2.00 each and was selling them for $1.75 each. His accountant asked how was he going to make a profit and the man responded, "We will make it up in volume". The accountant pressed on thinking the man was nuts. "Sir, how can you make money when you are selling the widgets for less than you are paying for them?" The man responded, "Well the market price for my widgets is $2.50 each. At $1.75 I sell a million of them per year. I buy them from my brother-in-law. Once I buy 1000, he pays me a volume incentive of $.75 for each widget I sell. So, I really make $.50 per widget or $500,000 per year." Clearly, he knows his numbers!

Assuming your endeavor is a For Profit strategy; all the fun and fulfillment or personal pride you glean from your business will be short lived if the numbers do not work. That is because your business will not sustain itself unless the profits are there.

Understanding the profit numbers is the bedrock on which you will build your business. Underneath the profit numbers are other numbers that must work in order to make profits. Productivity, capacities, market size, market share, cost to produce and start-up capital are just a few of the sets of numbers which must be understood before the profit numbers can be calculated. Maximizing each of these calculations is where the rubber meets the road. Your own innovations, strategies, vision, methodology and expectations will determine the extent to which you will get the most from your efforts. These do not have to be mountain-sized analyses, but they must be thorough enough to be accurate and reasonable. These factors and calculations will become part of your business plan.

It is imperative that you know how to calculate your numbers. You must be able to create the models of your business through spreadsheet analysis. Learn Excel and use it. Being able to create your own models insulates you from charlatans who, well-meaning or not, can corrupt your view of your business proposition.

You want to model in two different ways. I call them single contract and overall models. Single contract models look at the viability of creating one unit. If you are manufacturing pencils, it would be the cost to produce, cost to sell, cost to distribute against the sales price to determine the profit per unit. The overall model considers the overall business P&L. Using volume expectations and overall costs considering capacities related to staff and equipment. For example, you would consider how many pencils you can sell per month and how much revenue that would produce. You then look at manufacturing and distribution cost to determine how many people and how much equipment it would take to make the pencils. Then you would compare your staff's capacity and current equipment against ideal capacities. The uneven amount of sales each month or seasonally creates a difference in these resulting in uneven costs. So how the bottom line is managed requires using this model. Both models must be viable to determine the viability of a business proposition. You must be the resident expert on these numbers, no exceptions

Once you have internalized the numbers you will be able to make business decisions, modify strategies, make investments or raise capital for your business. You will also be less susceptible to schemes aimed at you. In a word, nobody can BS you about your business.

Module 3- Planning and Modeling

Lesson 3-2- Conservative approach to forecasting and budgeting

Even though this lesson is specific to starting your own business it may have some aspects helpful in your career especially a career change.

We all have lofty goals and expectations as to the success of our business. We also have an expectation as to the pace of the growth and short-term results. You should certainly write these down and plan your activities around achieving, if not exceeding, these goals. However, when initial budgeting and financial planning for the start-up of your business, a conservative approach is the only way to go. In order to build your plan and budget you must consider, amongst other things, sales, cash flow and cash requirements for at least the initial 24 months. You should be prepared for a worst-case scenario to test your ability to weather the naturally uneven pace of business, especially new ventures. It is a proven fact that most businesses either fail or at least take longer than planned to succeed. If you are not prepared for less or slower success you are setting yourself up for failure. It may be a wiser move to use various scenarios like 1) worst case, 2) expected, 3) better. This way you can make your plans accordingly for cash requirements, inventory, financial facilities, etc. Just like you do not want to run out of capital if things move slower than expected, you should also have a plan for more success than expected. The same strategy should be employed when it comes to expenses. You should have the cash to pay your bills at a higher rate than you expect as costs are always higher than planned. Higher than expected expenses coupled with slower than expected sales is the worst-case scenario and you should understand this and be prepared. Then only opportunity exists.

Once you have modeled the various scenarios and have secured the funding then and only then should you move on your plan. You should be vigilant in reviewing your results quarterly against your models. I would not recommend doing it more often as monthly blips may not yet be a trend. Your quarterly review may warn you to make changes to your plan, funding, etc.

These models do not have to be fancy or expensive software or advice. Learn Excel and build three spreadsheets. Take your time and try to include as much detail as possible. You will not be able to build these at one sitting. Indeed, even after you do have them built, take some time away from them and in a few days go back and validate and/or tweak the models. Using a conservative business plan, monitoring it, and making interim changes will be a determinant factor in your chances of success.

Module 3- Planning and Modeling
Lesson 3-3- Startup Finances

As discussed in previous lessons financing your new venture is an important piece to the puzzle. The cost and control of the start-up funds, how you invest the money and closely monitoring the expenditures are the main factors to consider regarding operating capital.

How much money do you need?

The first question is how much capital do you need to start your company. First, decide how you are entering this endeavor. It is a good strategy to commence on a part time basis in your spare time while maintaining your job to keep your cash flow level. There will be instances when you either cannot or prefer not going that slow.

Moving slower allows you to;
- Test the waters of your concept and vision. Testing in a less stressful situation while still maintaining your personal cash flow allows you to make better longer-term decisions. You can see flaws and adjustments without the risk of cash flow issues. Then when you are ready to make the jump you can be more confident in your chances of success.
- Test the profit model to be comfortable with the numbers. It is almost a guarantee that your original model will not capture all profits and all expenses. Doing this in a stress-free cash flow timeframe can save much capital once you jump in with both feet.
- Create a track record of sales and revenue to sharpen your business plan in terms of timing and amount of revenue during the first 24 months. This is important intelligence as it is critical that you have 24 months of cash flow in the bank before going full time. Having a track record already allows you to know how much money you need for business expenses, inventory and personal expenses.
- Create revenue that can be accumulated to self-fund the beginning months after you quit your job.

If you are jumping in right away;
- Have 24 months of expenses, both personal and business in the bank before starting. If you go with any less you are risking failure. Many great ideas for a business venture fail because they run out of money before the concept begins to return profits sufficient to sustain the owner's needs.

- First choice- Fund Yourself- It is by far a better strategy to use your own capital when starting your first venture. The requirement of repayment can be a financial burden that makes your venture more challenging and slow your cash flow. It also causes undo pressure on you to pay off the note, thus distracting you from your business at hand. I would recommend self-funding even if it means a postponement of the venture. If that is not possible, then make sure you borrow from a trusted source and do not give away your future business ownership in the long run. Family may be your best second option.

Start on the cheap, but...

You certainly must watch your pennies in your business as in your personal finances. Finding the lowest cost for the best equipment, supplies, etc., will help success come sooner. So, no extravagant spending. That does not mean that you should not spend money. Spend money on things that will best promote your success is prudent. You can look extravagant without actually being extravagant. Websites and social media are less expensive marketing strategies and should be done. But I still believe that person to person marketing create longer term relationships. Referral exchanges are good as long as you vet the groups as they are not all the same or as effective.

Watch the cash flow

- It is critical to always monitor the net cash flow and cash balances in your business. This is especially critical in the first 24 months. You should always know your cash position and your financial needs at the end of the month. Nobody will worry about this better than you and you must be on top of it at all time. Do not make any larger decisions due to one month's results. Look at the numbers monthly but rarely should you make large decisions without the benefit of at least a three-month trend.

In summary start-up finances are not a thing to take lightly and it is imperative that you do your homework. Your success rate will increase when your cash flow is working.

Module 4- Business Ethics

These are four truisms that capture my beliefs relating to Business Ethics. If you have long range goals for your business pay attention because poor ethics will doom your organization.

Make every decision as if it will be published in the Wall Street Journal. Too many times we see embarrassing revelations of people on TV or the internet. Each time we say, "What were they thinking?" The answer is, they weren't. People make decisions supposedly under confidential circumstances that give them a false sense of security that "nobody will ever know". Then when they are caught, they say they are sorry. We often wonder are they sorry they did it or sorry they were caught? When it comes to business ethics you should always assume that the news will come out. So, you should always think, "If this decision becomes public, what affect will it have on my family, my integrity, my business, my employees or my customers". When you use this filter, you can sleep well at night knowing that your decision will withstand the scrutiny of opinion.

If you are not sure it is ethical, it probably is not. I also call this the gut test. When making a decision I often verbalize to myself or someone else one of the options. Almost always I have a feeling in my stomach that tells me what I really think down deep. However, when it comes to deciding if something is ethical, or the right thing to do, I always say, "If I am not sure if it is wrong it probably is wrong." That is because when it is ethical, I always know.

The fish smells from the head. This old proverb means that if an organization is bad or unethical it means this trait is prevalent all the way up to the boss/owner. If an owner either does not lead by example or clearly speak out regarding ethics it will filter all the way down. It is just as bad to turn your head as it is to direct or condone unethical practices. Either way the stench will pervade your organization

It is not personal it is business. This has less to do with the decisions and more to do with how you decide amongst good decisions. Michael Corleone was right, making a decision that is best for the company should not be motivated on injuring or rewarding individuals. It should always be what is best for the greater good. That does not mean you should not concern yourself with the effect of the decision may have on others. It means it should not be the deciding factor. Indeed, several times in my career I actually recommended changing or closing my own department thus discontinuing my own job. Not easy to do, but I can tell you that it has always ended with me being in a better position afterward.

In Conclusion, critical thinking should always be made from a solid base of ethics

Module 5- Business Philosophy
Lesson 5-1- Manage with a long-term view, but…

In my experience, the companies that made their strategic decisions with a long-term view, had sustainable growth and continued success. Every time I saw a group making decisions with only short-term gain objectives, the group/company was gone in a few years or less. Managing in crisis mode with quick fixes is a characteristic of a poorly managed organization. Short term, rushed solutions usually are only band-aids and are almost always more expensive. Developing strategies whereby the organization recognizes annual profits but always builds annuity type income is important. You must feed the kids this year and create revenue to fund their college education in the future.

I witnessed way too much of this in my corporate career. You would expect that multi-national companies would make decisions with a longer-term view as they do not live month to month. This could not be further from the truth. I saw some of the worst decisions made by these corporations. Short term profits and long-term mistakes are regularly made. Most of them are hidden in their balance sheets, but they do slow the long-term success and affect employees and stockholders in the long run. Sometimes they even bring the company down. Sometimes they make compromises to make their stock price look better in a particular quarter. Even more insidious is when senior managers make short term profit boosting decisions that will most likely cost the company in the future in order to bolster their bid for a large promotion in the near-term. Time after time I saw this happen as they get the promotion amidst strong financials and then the next poor slob that gets their job is eventually mired in a financial crisis. The blame is always placed on the person in charge left holding the bag.

Managing for the long term is not often easy and in the short term usually reduces profits. This can be in the form of investing in infrastructure like systems and office space. This costs near term money, but can save money and efficiencies 200%, 300% or higher in the future. Sometimes investing in human capital is appropriate. Hiring and training employees ahead of expected growth can avoid service issues in the future. It also signals to the employees and competitors that you are forward thinking and expecting success.

While it is vital to make decisions for the long term, you must not forget the short term. When modeling your business, a thoughtful business plan that analyzes the annual cash flow needs of the organization. This will help make those short term and long-term decisions. Similarly, when making strategic decisions both the short-term needs and the long-term sustainable growth considerations should be addressed. Only in crisis mode should it be necessary to only focus on short term rewards.

Module 5 - Business Philosophy

Lesson 5-2- Reputation is everything

Everyone has a reputation whether it is personal or business related. Unfortunately, people make decisions based upon one's reputation even if it is untrue. It is not fair when one's reputation can be marred by a simple allegation without corroboration. In our society of drive by news viewed on a smartphone we see an undo level of non-understanding. If you only read the headlines you are not learning the whole story, or worse, being misled.

On a personal level, when one has a certain negative reputation, many people will avoid the person without even learning about the person for themselves. This precludes some potentially wonderful friendships from forming. Some people avoid these people so as to not be judged through guilt by association. This is often unfortunate.

In the business world a person's or business's reputation is all important. Obviously, potential customers will avoid dealing with companies with a bad reputation so as to not be victimized by an unscrupulous company. So, this stigma will cost the company much revenue and could result in their failure. It is just as devastating from a recruiting talent perspective. Quality people will not apply for a job or respond to a recruiting effort from a company with a bad reputation. Consequently, it is impossible to grow your company with quality people when you have a bad reputation. This will doom a company.

Of course, the best advice is to never allow a bad reputation to be formed. How do you do that?

- *Be a person or business of good character.* Conduct yourself and your business with sound ethics and morality. Continually reinforce character to you people. Treat employees, friends, family and customers fairly. Clearly communicate plans, changes, issues, etc. to everyone. Insist upon open communications both incoming and outgoing. Never allow any retaliations to be made to anyone providing information or reporting bad behavior within the company. Be open with friends and family and welcome feedback without recourse.
- *Surround yourself with quality people that value and practice those characteristics above.*
- *When conflict arises, as it always does, deal with it immediately, openly and from a point of view of high character.* Do not waiver

from your core beliefs and do not compromise your integrity. People are always watching and evaluating you and change or affirm their sense of your reputation. When they go low, you go high. Your customer service department is one of the most important pieces of your organization. What they do and say, how well they are trained and how committed they are to a positive customer experience is ultimately going to determine your company's reputation in the marketplace. And finally, follow up and monitor the execution of the agreed upon course of action until it's conclusion.

A good reputation can take years to develop. However, a bad reputation can come about instantaneously. And once you have a bad reputation it will take a long time to turn around. So how do you turn a bad reputation around? It is a clear as this.

- Avoid situations that can later be misconstrued or mischaracterized.
- Recognize and admit the errors or prove their untruth immediately within the company or you personally.
- Follow the 3 steps above and prove that change has occurred. Make sure there is not a chance of a repeat of the bad actions.
- Take the temperature of opinion often to see that progress is being made

On the other hand, a good reputation is one to be coveted and protected. It is also the best marketing campaign in the world. Word of mouth recommendations and endorsements create more potential customers/friends than spending a boatload of marketing money. Pay close attention to your reputation in this social networking world. Yelp and other opinion sights must be monitored constantly to make sure you know what people are saying. Then you can quickly deal with any issues in real time.

You must also be plugged into your employee's opinions of you and the company so you always know what the sentiment is like. Create an open forum or an environment of open discussion will help you here. Of course, there is always recreational complaining. Officers in the service say that if you do not hear any recreational complaining by sergeants you should be concerned. If there is silence then they might be planning a mutiny. You must be able to distinguish between a personal opinion and what is common belief. This can only be determined if you are plugged into your people. This is vital to a healthy company.

Module 5- Business Philosophy
Lesson 5-3- What I Learned from my Mentors

Cliff - "Smile when you are on the phone, they will hear it on the other end." You cannot fake sincerity

George - "Never bring a problem to your boss without having one or more solutions to offer." Monkey on his back.

Hank - "Deliver bad news directly and quickly without long commiseration." Pull the band aid off all at once.

Charlie - "If you know the underlying numbers you will understand the business." If you do not you will fail.

Dave - "Get out in front of conflicts, controversies, etc. Confront the people and resolve things now"

I was fortunate to have several mentors throughout my career. While my parents and the church taught me right from wrong and life lessons like;

- Do the right thing, even if it is not easy
- Take responsibility for yourself and your actions
- The Ten Commandments
- Family is everything

I have taken many things from my business mentors that helped me shape and ultimately find success, in my career.

Here are just a few;

Cliff- The Best Salesman I ever met
My Real Estate/Finance career started with my meeting Cliff. I was in college and pumping gas at a gas station in Hollywood, Fl. This man came in for gas on a regular basis. He was always nice, jovial and personable to me and always had a smile on his face. He worked as a sales agent at a Real Estate firm down the street. He spoke to me about his job and the wonderful career it made. He was a retired New York City firefighter and was proud of it. He was still young and I always thought of him as I finished my college time and was thinking about what I wanted to do long term. I had several other jobs in between but nothing that interested me as a career. I

remembered Cliff and the career he described. I found that he had opened his own Brokerage firm. I met with him to discuss my thought of starting a career in Real Estate. He highly recommended that I consider this option as he felt I would be successful. I asked him if he had a formal training program. He said he did not but could help me himself. I then met with another firm and they promised me a complete training program. Even though I liked Cliff much better, I felt I should get the best training. I went to work with the other firm. They assigned me to renting dilapidated homes owned by a doctor. There was not only no training as promised, but the more I observed their business practices the more I sensed an atmosphere of sleaze. One day one of the other agents, an older man, took me aside and told me that I should get out of there as he was doing because of the shady nature of management. I took his advice and called Cliff. He said he knew I would be back. He told me that he never lied and when I asked him about formal training, he told the truth. However, he agreed to take me under his wing. Upon joining his firm and spending time with him one thing was very apparent. He was a consummate and natural sales person. He worked hard and truly liked people. I learned much about Real Estate and selling from Cliff. Of the many the things I learned there was one thing that I used every day throughout my career. I would watch him answer the phone, especially customer inquiries. We would be having a serious discussion on a topic, but when the phone rang, he picked up the phone and the biggest grin came over his face. He just lit up. And it remained until he hung up. After a while I asked him about his smile during sales calls. He told me this and I remember it like it was yesterday. "When you answer the phone smile widely. The person can hear your smile and are immediately open to your conversation." I just had to try this. The next call came in and I put on a big smile and said, "Hello". Well it was amazing the response I received from the caller. I did this every day throughout my career. God Bless that man. We lost him much too soon. He taught me many things, but this was the best.

George- The most instinctive business manager I ever met
After 4 years working as a mortgage loan officer, I went to work for the 5th largest S&L in the state. During that time, I was fortunate to learn a great deal about the mortgage business from creating mortgage notes to correspondent lending. Long story short, the bank ended up being part of the S&L meltdown in the early eighties. When the bank failed, Citibank purchased the assets and people. The division of Citi that was placed in charge of our bank was the second mortgage division. They were based in St. Louis. The senior managers were experienced sales people and managers. I had several good managers and progressed well. I soon began

reporting to George. He was a seasoned second mortgage guy that was with the company Citi bought to create this division. George was a street level veteran and while he was fair, he did not hold anyone's hand. I watched him handle street level issues and senior management. He dealt with the former in a swift and direct way and the latter in a smooth, but impatient manner. He had no patience with senior people that tried to manage with no street level experience. He was a bit intimidating to me at first, but we worked well together. He taught me many things, especially handling the corporate politics. The best lesson he taught me was how to manage up. Meaning how to help your boss look good and to get things done through your boss that you believe are in everyone's best interest. The number one tactic I learned was taught to me during a particularly stressful time. I had been promoted into a position and the department was a mess. I was struggling being able to determine the best way to navigate through the corporate world. One day I had a particularly desperate situation. I finally jumped up and went to see George. I told him what the big problem was and waited for his sage advice. When I finished, he just looked at me and said, "and?". I said "and what?" He said and what do you suggest we do? I told him, "that is why I came to see you." He said these words. "Never come to your manager with a problem without bringing at least two possible solutions." I thought that was his way of getting out of helping me. In a way it was, but there were two reasons as I later came to understand.

When you seek your own solutions first, you spend the time thinking through the problem and either figure it out yourself or at least understand the issue and the alternatives.

When you handle problems like this you come off to your superior as a professional who thinks through issues and a person that makes their life easier without them having to come up with every decision. Also, you do not throw the monkey of burden from your back to theirs. I later read a book entitled "The One Minute Manager Meets the Monkey" by Ken Blanchard. This dealt with just this. Not allowing others to throw their problems on your back and in turn taking it from theirs. I have used that ever since as an employee, a manager and a father. Thanks George.

Hank – The direct approach is best

Soon after working for George, I was moved under Hank managing several diverse departments. I recollect overseeing Portfolio management, Employee loans, local servicing, and a couple others. While I had managed small groups of mostly sales before that, I had never managed many staffers. It came to pass that the bank went through some tough times and a massive reorganization was ordered. I have chronicled this situation in full in Module 8, Lesson 8-4. But in short, Hanks was a veteran senior manager and taught me how to best handle very serious personnel situations like layoffs and firings. Unfortunately, I have had to lay off way too many people after that day in my career. But I handled each one as Hank taught me. It was the best way.

Charlie, the smartest man I ever met

While still at Citibank while I was running the Secondary marketing department a new Treasurer for the Bank was brought on board. I was told that my department was now going to report to the Treasury division and I was to report to Charlie. Charlie was a 56 yr. old, 32-year Citi veteran who had worked in headquarters in Manhattan as well as many overseas assignments including England, Australia and the Philippines. A St Johns' graduate with 9 children, he was well respected by the long time Bankers. The word was he was a high ranking Citibanker under the prior worldwide CEO, Walter Wriston. Among his duties, Charlie was the person who delivered the corporate numbers and performance for the Board of Directors and at the Annual Shareholder's meeting. He was the numbers guy. In those days he was a rival of the new worldwide CEO John Reed. Charlie was rumored to have been up for that job. When John became CEO Charlie was passed over.

I met Charlie and he was initially an unassuming slight man and did not appear very healthy. But soon it was apparent to me that he was simply brilliant. Not only was he nearly a savant when it came to numbers and balance sheets but he was so corporately intuitive and was always ahead of his peers in preparation and instincts. In all of his experience, he had never been involved in residential mortgage lending. When my department came under his responsibility, he met with me and discussed our new association. He made a deal with me that was so much more important to me than it could have ever been to him. He said that if I would teach him the mortgage business, he would teach me the numbers underlying all businesses as well as the corporate reporting. He also taught me the importance of preparation. The following three years was the equivalent to me of a Master in Business and Finance. He was a tireless worker and would regularly stay beyond 9:30 PM. He would always expect me to stay also. I was always a morning person and I would get to the office at 7:30 – 8:00 AM. He came in around 9:30 AM. So, I was putting in 12+ hours daily. But I never complained as I was absorbing knowledge that prepared me for the rest of my career. The number one reality I learned from Charlie was the following;

"Always know the underlying numbers of the business to determine where the profits and the threats are located. "Know the numbers and you can never be snowed."

Charlie was taken from us much too soon a couple of years later. Simply the smartest guy I ever met.

Dave- Be a straight shooter deal with issues now

My relationship with Dave started as peers, later I worked for him and eventually and still today we are best of friends. While I was working for Charlie running the secondary marketing my group controlled the pricing of the mortgage loans. Dave was the head of our second mortgage division. He was a seasoned mortgage guy with many years with the bank. We sometimes had difficult decisions to make on pricing which affected Dave's production but he was always respectful and professional and we liked each other. After a couple of years things changed in the Bank and our department was centralized to St. Louis. I had no interest in moving and wanted to get back into mortgage sales anyway. Dave offered me a job managing the most productive second mortgage office in the country. Great boss and we developed a close relationship. Later, after we both left the Bank, Dave reached out to me and brought me into his next company. We flourished and thanks to Dave's offer, we helped create a nationwide $6 Billion organization. Thanks to Dave and this success I was able to retire in the fashion I could only have once dreamed. We spent countless hours together and early on I saw Dave as someone with the highest integrity. That trait manifested itself in how he handled conflict, betrayal, unscrupulous behavior, etc. Dave would get on the issue now. Not tomorrow or later today. He would get in front of the person and confront them bluntly and firmly. Early on I sometimes cringed at how confrontational it became. That was partially me as I was always more averse to confrontation. But soon I saw how effective his approach was and more importantly how honest it was. You never had to guess where you stood with Dave. He would say, "Get in front of it now and it will be resolved sooner and better". Thanks, my friend.

By the way, mentors do not have to be your superiors. I have learned much from people that I worked with and who worked for me. There are others not documented here that mentored me and showed the way and I thank all of them. Having the benefit of quality people in my business life was a major factor in whatever level of success I achieved. You should always pay attention to those with more experience and/or more success than you. You will learn things they do not teach you in school.

Module 5- Business Philosophy

Lesson 5-4- Making Career Decisions

At the beginning of your career you must decide what kind of work you want to do. I highly recommend you take the advice in Module 8 on job fit. Take the Myers Briggs test yourself to confirm your personality tendencies. Then decide on a career that fits you.

Over the course of your career you will have many opportunities to move into a different job within your company or moving to another company. These are some of the most exciting and terrifying times and very well can be life changing, both positive and negative.

There are many models that attempt to help one analyze options when making career decisions. For smaller decisions, once I have gone through my analysis and think I have a decision I utilize the following "Gut Test". I say out loud to myself or a significant other what I have decided to do. Invariably, as soon as I say it, I get a feeling in my stomach telling me if it is good or bad. Make sure it is just not fear or nervousness about the move. But if it truly gives you a bad feel in your stomach, review your thought process because you missed something. For major decisions however affecting all aspects of my life it falls short. The gut test measures what you would like to do. It does not consider what you should do. As a result, it does not cover all the bases.

My Process

For real career decisions I have used an analytical blueprint throughout my career that works for me. You must take your time and really do an in-depth review of each item. I look at each option under the microscope of three perspectives in no particular order;

I examine the opportunity as to its effect on;
- My Career development- Does this job advance my standing in my profession? Does this job provide an expanded knowledge base? Does this job improve my resume for future plans? Am I ready for this job? If it is a move to another company, is it a quality organization? Are they perceived as ethical? Do they treat their employees properly?
- My Financial needs- Does this job result in at least a similar or increased income now or the near future? Does it provide bonuses? What are the chances of earning the bonuses? Does it position me for my next job earning substantially more income? Are the earnings

stable? Is the company stable? I have taken positions with the same or slightly less income only when the other two factors are extraordinarily positive and it does not risk me not having enough income to pay the bills even short term.
- My Family life- Is this job going to take me away from my family so much that it could be detrimental? Are we going to have to move to take this job, and if so, what is the impact on my family? Will it impact my spouse's career plans?

I will evaluate each of the questions above and then rely on the following advice. I will state this emphatically, if the effect on any of the above three considerations is negative, DO NOT TAKE THE JOB.

If any one of these is not positive, you will eventually regret the move and possibly irreversibly injure your career, finances or family. I believe in this analysis as it has worked over my career and those of many that have asked for my counsel on these decisions. Once you have decided, it still is not a bad idea to use the gut test just to make sure.

Now I would like to say a word about excessive job changes vs. being loyal to your company and sticking it out. First of all, if you apply the above tests for every move, you will not be job hopping in the negative sense. You will have thought through the move and should be good until a better opportunity comes along. Do not change jobs for change sake. It does not look good on your resume and usually does not further your career, finances or family life. Conversely, do not live in misery for any longer than you have absolutely must. In today's world, the concept of loyalty and quietly waiting your turn are long gone. I am not saying you must not pay your dues. Moving too fast does not allow you time to be proficient in the job. Most people believe they are ready for the next job before they actually are prepared. As I discussed in Module 1, learn your business cold, suffer through several business cycles and be able to make decisions from instinct before looking for the next growth opportunity. However, once you are ready, I no longer prescribe to the theory that your company will look out for you and give you the next opportunity. Sometimes they do and that is wonderful. However, do not turn down a real outside opportunity, once you have vetted it as above, for the sake of being loyal. I have long since believed that, in business, if you want loyalty buy a dog. You should also be auditioning and communicating with your management that you feel you are ready for another challenge. But do not pass up a real one outside in the meantime.

Module 5- Business Philosophy

Lesson 5-5 - Decision Making- Not a democratic process

As a business manager or leader, part of a prudent decision-making process is soliciting the thoughts and opinions of your team, peers and/or respected friends. Nobody is smart enough to have the right answer or understand all of the issues on larger type decisions. Also, as a leader, one should allow others to feel part of the process. This is as much for the team's unity as it is for the leader to have all the facts in front of them to aid in the decision-making process. Studies and presentations can be solicited if the decision is of larger importance. A careful review of all input by the ultimate decision maker is required.

However, I have seen decision makers abdicate their responsibility and put the matter up to a vote by subordinates. Large decisions should not be a democratic process. I do believe there are times and levels of decisions for which this democratic process may be prudent. These are low risk decisions and usually with a less mature team as a coaching tool. Once the risk levels rise a bit but still not too high, I have seen leaders allow a vote but cleverly place their thumb on the scale. Typically, if the leader sees a decision heading in the wrong direction, they provide their opinion in a way not to dictate but add to the discussion. Often this leads the group to the best decision. The abdication I am referring to is related to larger decisions with higher risk. At the end of the process only one person should make the final decision, the leader. The reason for this autocratic process is simple. If the decision goes bad it always reflects always directly on the leader. Their neck is on the line. I have subscribed to a view that I do not allow someone else to control my success. I am the one responsible for my successes and failures. This is not to say that a leader should not usually consult with his folks. They should go through the process described above. But one must always be up front with the team by stating that while they welcome the input, this decision must be finally made by the manager/leader. This is an honest way to approach these decisions.

Another point to be made here is part of the deliberation and research must be for the purpose of uncovering unintended consequences. How this decision will affect others and how they may affect future plans and decisions. Failure to take unintended consequences into account can transform an otherwise good decision a bad one and damage the business. Remember always try to take a long-term view.

Section 2- Process

Module 6- Recruiting and Hiring

Lesson 6-1- Surround Yourself with Smart Hard-Working People- Then try to Keep Up!

Any General will tell you that they are only as good as their soldiers. No matter how intelligent and engaged the leader is, nothing gets done unless someone makes it happen. When recruiting people for your organization you should look for those candidates that are even sharper than you. They should possess the work ethic and commitment necessary for the position. Beyond that your choices should be made with few other filters. This means you should bring in people with varied perspectives and do not just hire like-minded people.

I have always looked for folks that have positive characteristics that I do not necessarily possess. For instance, I feel I can, given time, see the big picture and formulate a proper strategy to a fast-moving situation. However, I am not the best at on the spot perspective and shooting from the hip. Sometimes that characteristic is required. So, I always have at least one key person around me that can do this. Hiring your key folks with a complimentary set of skills and capabilities is vital for a high functioning team.

Do not hire "YES" people. It certainly can be good for the ego when those around you agree with you. However, nobody is that smart. You must have people that will challenge the status quo bringing diverse perspectives on the business. This will create an ever-changing and ever-growing organization always striving for improvement.

A mixture of personalities is important within your staff. You need that hard charging person to knock down walls, but you also need that person that can pick up the pieces and put everything in its new place. You need people always watching the bottom line but always need the folks that have the customer's perception in mind.

Managing a group such as this is a challenge. You must have an open-mindedness that can process the varied approaches even if you do not initially agree with them. Most people have good qualities and not so good qualities. In business and in life you should surround yourself with quality people that are primarily decent individuals. Once you have that, you can coach, counsel or even accept certain parts of their personalities that you do not like or agree with but do not injure others or have anything to do with results. You must also play referee at times as these different thinking folks will often disagree and it actually can get ugly. Your job is to make sure everyone plays fair and is heard.

As I reflect on the many teams I have been involved in, I realize that best of them were filled with the smartest, diverse and most passionate people. It is one of the keys to success.

Probably one of my most successful teams ever was definitely my most challenging group. I was in charge of a team that was responsible for packaging closed mortgage loans and selling them into the secondary market. This was during the time when the securitization, or bundling of groups of loans, was becoming the preferred method. I was given the task of developing a team to pass these loans thus creating much of the profit for the mortgage business. Actually, when I was charged with this challenge, I had not ever sold loans in the securitized fashion. The first thing I had to do was find people who knew how to do this. My first hire was a young man who had been trained by the bank in capital markets. Wall street, trading, etc. He was very smart and possessed another trait I needed which was quick, on the spot and usually on the mark analysis. He was a good person but not the most open, engaging and warm individual. But together we developed the models and process for selling loans. I next needed an operations person that knew the mechanics of packaging loans for sale. I found a person that was very experienced in this field. She was a hard worker with an excellent work ethic. She was smart and pragmatic. She had a strong personality and would not back down from anybody. Again, a good person. I then brought over with me a person I had worked closely with in many capacities during my career. She was a great organizer with an engaging personality that could manage people flawlessly. She also possessed the quick mind to analyze situations rapidly and additionally had a street-smart sense to see what may lie underneath a situation. She was not just a good person; she was a great person that stayed with me for much of my career. I owe much of my success to her and we remain friends to this day. These folks hired folks under them and we had a 10-12-person team. I also managed a few other groups at the same time, so I had to rely upon this team of leaders. Together we created the capability to package and sell loans with the best profit and fastest turn-times in the bank. Even better than the huge teams in our home office. My challenge was keeping them from killing each other, especially the trader and the operations person. The Operations person reported to the Trader. They just did not get along and were often at odds. Even in this environment, we were very successful. Despite our success, the day to day interactions were volatile. We had such deadlines and some huge sales and I had the keep it all together. It got so bad that I actually had to separate the two and have the operations person report to me directly. This made no sense looking at the organization chart, but sometimes that does not matter. This worked, as I acted as a buffer and they eventually began working well together. As time went on, we formed a great group of friends and some of my fondest memories was this time with them.

This only worked because I found smart people who were also good souls and allowed them to flourish.

Module 6- Recruiting and Hiring

Lesson 6-2- Job Match is Paramount

Square Peg- Round Hole

Hiring the right person based upon the match of personality and job is the single most important tactic in the hiring process. This is especially true when you are looking at candidates with a limited amount of experience in the job function. If they have had several jobs performing the function over the last year or two you should pay particular attention to job match.

People are complex beings with a combination of personality types. Indeed, the Myers Briggs* model has 16 separate types and there are many variations amongst these. We do not have to be psychologists to hire the right people. But knowing their basic personalities will help you match a person to a job. I see many young people in college studying for a degree in a field that they may never be successful in because they have not considered their personality.

There is a simple test that looks at just four personality traits that takes 10 minutes to perform. It will give you enough information to support your decision to hire without being complicated. The following website provides this test. http://www.123test.com/disc-personality-test/

This test looks at four characteristics
1. Dominance
2. Influence
3. Steadiness
4. Compliance

Each person will score with a certain percentage in each characteristic. But remember that the percentages matter and often people have similar percentages in multiple areas. However, people usually have a dominant characteristic and it should be considered for job match.

High Dominance is a characteristic of entrepreneurs, senior managers and leaders. If you are looking for someone to groom for leadership roles this would be a place to start.

High Influence is a characteristic of sales people, attorneys, negotiators and the like. If you are hiring someone to bring in business this is your person.

High Steady is a characteristic of an office manager, an organizer or a person to clean up behind the High Influence and High Dominance people.

They are not going to sell, create or drive an organization, but without these people nothing gets done.

High Compliance is a characteristic of an underwriter, auditor, quality control person or accountant. They will not lead, sell or organize but will keep you in business with solid calculated information and decisions.

These are simplistic examples and you should always pay attention to their next highest trait as often people can temper or expand their effectiveness tapping into their secondary trait. For example, I measured out nearly equal in both High Influence(sales) and High Steady(operations). I was fortunate in that I was able to compete and flourish in both of these types of roles. It also gave me perspectives into one group while I was managing the other. Most senior managers have a second trait in which they are at least above average.

Fitting the square peg into the square hole can save thousands of dollars and avoid missing business opportunities.

Module 6- Recruiting and Hiring

Lesson 6-3- Make sure Managers can Manage

The best way to teach this concept is by analogy. If you list the most productive and successful coaches or managers in all sports, a majority of them were not superstar athletes or top players. In fact, very few superstar players ever entered the coaching side of their game or if they did, enjoyed much success. There are a few exceptions, but in most cases, even superstars that enjoyed minimal success were seldom good teachers of the game. Let's look at some examples;

Top 10 Baseball players- Babe Ruth, Willie Mays, Ted Williams, Hank Aaron, Ken Griffey Jr, Mickey Mantle, Lou Gehrig, Ty Cobb, Brooks Robinson and Roger Clemens

Top 10 NFL Players- Jim Brown, Jerry Rice, Joe Montana, Walter Payton, Lawrence Taylor, Johnny Unitas, John Elway, Dick Butkus, Reggie White and Dan Marino

Top 10 NBA Players- Michael Jordan, Kareem Abdul Jabbar, Magic Johnson, Bill Russell, Larry Bird, Wilt Chamberlain, Hakeem Olajuwon, Oscar Robertson, David Robinson and Jerry West

All have one thing in common. They either never coached, of if they did, they were not considered successful.

You would have to agree that this is counterintuitive. You would think that superstars would make great coaches. After all they were the best, why would they not be able to teach others to be the same. I am not saying that these people are not role models and that many people have not emulated their style, training and work habits. They just did not want or could not succeed managing others.

I have found this to also be the case in sales people. For years, we would promote our superstar sales people to be managers. They were thought to be able to transfer their success to teams of others. The vast majority of the time this was a huge mistake. Not only were they not good at motivating others we also lost our best sales person in the field.

So why is this true? I believe there are at least two factors relative to superstars that preclude them from being superstar managers.

Natural ability- Most of these individuals have natural, instinctive qualities/skill levels that, for the most part, cannot be replicated or transferred. A natural athlete hardly ever needed to learn how to be a great athlete. It came naturally. Natural sales people find it easy to create and keep customers. It is difficult for them to teach it to others and even harder to instill those qualities in others because they never had to learn it themselves.

Personality- most highly successful sales people and athletes are of a personality type that is very inwardly focused. They derive their pleasure from doing, not teaching. Most do not have the patience to manage and will not tolerate a lack of success, effort or talent as they have always been successful and talented.

So, who are good managers? Let's look at the best in sports in no particular order;

- Don Shula- average player for the Cleveland Browns
- Tommy Lasorda- minor league first baseman
- Vince Lombardi- short NFL career
- Jim Leyland- minor leaguer
- Bill Belichick- Unheralded NFL career
- John Wooden- unknown as basketball player

Why are they so good as coaches/mangers?

Lack of natural athletic ability- because of this, the game did not come easy to them. They had to work twice as hard to keep up. They had to study to stay ahead and their work ethic had to be superior.

Personality- They all had a teaching knack that came from their personality. They were able to relate to the average players without the superior athletic abilities of the superstars. And finally, they mostly had a drive to create and succeed as a team.

So where are your best sales managers for instance? You should start with those that are at least average in sales. You cannot use someone who is clueless in meeting customer's needs and the work it takes to sell. If you look within a sales team you will look for people with the characteristic skills to be successful managers.

- Organizational skills- are a requirement because they must be able to manage the process for others that lack the skills.
- Knack/desire to teach- is a must as they will spend much of their time coaching and teaching their people.
- Persuasive negotiator- because they must be able to deal with personnel issues, customer disputes, etc.

- Superior work ethic- is particularly vital as they will be responsible for an entire team not just themselves.
- Team player- as they must rally teams together for the common good

The lesson here is simple. Do not be so anxious to promote your sales superstar to manager. You are most likely going to have a failing team under them and lose the sales numbers from the former star. Look for those moderately successful people with the traits necessary to teach, coach and lead.

Module 6- Recruiting and Hiring
Lesson 6-4- Role of a Sales Manager or Business Owner

I use the example of a sales manager, but this can apply to any manager or especially and business owner. They must have the talent, experience, personality and drive to support his/her role which includes the following job requirements;

1. Direct
2. Recruit
3. Train
4. Market

Let's take these individually.

Direct- A professional sales manager must have the ability to manage. That sounds obvious, but many times a really good sales person is promoted to sales manager without regard to their acuity to manage people. However, those with the personality and skill set required to be a manager who also possess sales skills are the most effective sales managers. While many manager roles do not necessarily require hands on experience on the exact job of those they manage, sales managers most often require previous experience. That is because of the fact that sales people are just different. They think differently, work differently and are motivated differently than staff members. Many are just quirky. I say that affectionately as I sold most of my career.

Many years ago, after having been a salesperson and spending several years managing staff people, I was offered a promotion to manage a sales group. I believed that with my experience in managing people, this should be simple. I remember going to one of my mentors prior to beginning the job. George was an old finance company veteran and had managed entire sales forces as well as entire businesses. I said, "George, I have a great opportunity". I added, "managing sales people should be no different than managing staff as I have been doing, right?". George looked at me for a second and just laughed. He said to come to see him in sixty days and ask him again. I assumed my new role as branch manager of the number one mortgage sales branch in all of Citibank`. This office was comprised of seasoned people who had enjoyed success for some time. I knew most of them from meetings and such in the past. I walked into the office the first day. I thought it was a smart thing to do to meet with the group first and then to meet with them individually. I called a meeting for 11 AM. There were a few grumbles but I paid no attention. I went into the meeting room at 10:55. Nobody was there. Now it was 11 and one person strolled in. By 11:10 all but two were there. I sent someone out to check and the final two got there at 11:20. I started talking and within 7 minutes the first person was looking at their watch and most others were not exactly focused on my incredible thoughts. I ended the meeting at 11:30 and they bolted out the door. Nothing nasty, just otherwise focused. I then turned my attention to the individual meetings. I started with Mary. She was a 16 veteran and was the number one sales person in the entire country and had been for several years. She was not only a perennial President's club member, but was later the first member of the Hall of Fame. I knew her casually. Mary walked into my office, smacking gum and smiling. I had prepared a question that would convey my willingness to support her and help in an any way required. I said, "Mary, you are an icon in the Bank and clearly the leader of this sales group." I continued, "Mary I want to ask you to tell me what exactly is the most important thing I can do to help you guys?" She looked at me, smiled and said, "Just stay out of our way." My face must have dropped momentarily, but I tried not to show any shock. I said that we would continue to chat over time and ended the meeting. I immediately closed the door to my office and called George and told him what had happened. He laughed for five minutes and finally said, "I guess you see that managing sales people is going to be a new challenge." He was so right. Fortunately, I was able to develop an amazing rapport with the group and that team continued their success.

There are many stories like this. So, suffice it to say, managing sales people is different. Understanding that is vital to success.

Recruit- A professional sales manager will only be successful if they can continually find the right sales people to join the team. It is just a fact that there is more turnover in a sales force compared to a group of staff members. It is a full-time job. You should constantly be on the lookout for talent. Trade shows, business mixers, and simply word of mouth are always best. Asking your customers who are the best sales people they see as our competition is very revealing and a great lead for new folks. Once you identify them it is important that you and your organization is recognized as players and have an array of products and compensation plans to compete. Otherwise you are always playing catch up. You and your company's reputation are most important when playing in the big leagues. Recruit always.

Train- A professional sales manager must be able to teach. They should be able to teach, monitor and coach their people on products as well as techniques. That is why the sales manager should always be a former line sales person. There is no substitution for the experience and credibility that experience brings.

M*arketing*- Your sales managers must always be great promoters of the company and their sales people. They must also be able to train their people on how to use the sales tools provided by the organization. Too often, amazing marketing tools are never utilized by the sales people. It is the job of the manager to make sure they know how to use these tools and their sales people are trained to use them. Finally, they must make sure they actually use them every day.

Module 6- Recruiting and Hiring
Lesson 6-5- The Rule of Three

I have rarely made a bad hiring decision when I was able to witness the candidate doing their job without them knowing I was watching. Similarly, in sales, I would just need one ride along day to have a very good picture of their chances for success with our organization. I would rarely be wrong. You can see work habits, organizational skills, energy, verbal skills, multi-tasking, business ethics and more by just being there. I could also gain a good perspective by watching sales people at trade shows or other events. However, you are rarely afforded the opportunity of a pre-hire ride along or seeing them in action. That is why in the vast majority of instances I would ride along with sales people hired by my managers in their first three weeks. Even though they were already on board, I could get a good sense of how they handle themselves in sales situations, how well known they are by their customers and if they are well liked by clients. I was rarely wrong once I had spent the time. But if the hire was a mistake, it was too late to avoid the time and expense of hiring a person that does not make it. On-boarding a new employee often cost several thousand dollars. So, mistakes on several employees is problematic at best.

We did employ some techniques in the hiring process that increased the odds of making the right decision. I received excellent training while at Citibank. We actually had "college level" training at least once per year. Often it was at a university. One of my favorites was a week we spent on "Recruiting and Selecting". One of the strategies I learned there was the "Rule of Three".

Three people interview a candidate

Three times

In Three different settings

- *Three people* allows for a wider range of viewpoints and personal impressions. Afterward, I would meet with the other two interviewers to discuss impressions and observations and recommendations.
- *Three times* allows opportunity to more deeply get into the persons talents, ethics, philosophies, etc.
- *Three different* settings also allowed a deeper view in sometimes more relaxed or comfortable settings like a restaurant. Seeing them

in different venues can usually allow you to see more sides of their personalities.

Typically, the other two interviewers only participated in one interview. But that was not set in stone.

After going through the above you will have a greater understanding of the individual in preparation for the other steps necessary to make a good decision. Nothing is full proof but at least when you start with this you have more confidence moving to the next steps.

There are so many other factors and techniques that should be utilized. Indeed, an entire book could be written on this subject. For instance, different types of candidates like, an entry level candidate that is not an experienced person in the field, would bring "job fit" issues into play.

Module 6- Recruiting and Hiring
Lesson 6-6- Due Diligence

Due diligence on researching the background of the candidate is vital. I always felt that asking for a person's personal and business references was a foolish endeavor. After all, who would provide you with a name of someone who would give them a bad reference? I would however look at the people they used as references to gain some insight as to type of people the candidate feels is an impressive reference. Once in a while I would call one. But most of the time I would pass.

On the other hand, calling previous employers can be very revealing. The first challenge is to get to their manager, not HR. HR will never give you anything but boiler plate responses that tell you nothing. I often ask the candidate for their direct manager's contact information. Even in speaking with their manager, in today's litigious and PC world, people are often reticent to say anything bad about a former employee. So rarely do you get an explicit negative reference. You must listen for what they do not say. You can get a feeling from their voice or inflection how they feel about the person. Initially you must also have very specific questions that are objective rather than subjective. This means production levels, meeting timelines or goals, etc. This way you can get into a warming conversation in which you can later inject more subjective questions that reveal more about the person. One trick I have used when I am not getting a candid perspective is to ask them simply this. "If this person were available would you rehire them?" Many times, they fumble around saying yes or say "not sure" or sometimes they actually say no. This question is less onerous for the manager and can sometimes work.

By far, the most effective strategy to obtaining very accurate intelligence involves creating a network of fellow managers within your industry with which you share candid, unfiltered information. I developed relationships with most of our competitors. Usually they are similar level people. I developed these over the years by meeting them at trade shows or conferences and by just calling them up. They want the same thing you do. A candid evaluation from someone you trust. You must provide the quality feedback you would expect to them so that the trust can be developed. Once you have this network, you will most always have top notch intelligence about your candidate. This strategy has saved me countless hiring mistakes. It also allowed me to make some great friends among competitors. Many of whom I later hired or worked with.

The work done in this step of the recruiting and hiring process will determine your success rate. Do your due diligence!

Module 6- Recruiting and Hiring

Lesson 6-7- The Cost of Making a Bad Hire

Hiring the wrong person is one of the most expensive mistakes a business can make. The expense involved in just getting to the hiring decision includes;

- Finding candidates can cost you service fees like for "Indeed" or "Monster.com"
- You pay a head hunter fee
- Cost of bringing candidate to office for multiple interviews. Often means airfare, hotels, etc.
- Your time and that of your managers to meet with candidate and meeting to discuss candidates

Then when you decide to hire the wrong person, the costs continue;
- HR must prepare paperwork, contracts, etc.
- The person must go through some form of training and in many cases, it can mean airfare, hotel, meals for multiple days
- The staff's time in actually training them. The salary paid to the new employee until they are productive on the job
- Time evaluating performance, and if below expectations, meeting and retraining costs. If they fail, you have missed opportunity of having a productive employee for the 2-3 months they are onboard.
- Then, you have to start over.

In my last job, we estimated that the average bad hire in Sales would cost between $6,000 and $10,000 each in real dollars.

Finally, there is the possibility of internal disruption, lowering of morale, people conflicts, weakening company performance and customer mistreatment. This happens all too often and, although it is difficult to quantify, it can be far more expensive than the actual costs above.

As you can see, recruiting and hiring is a risky and expensive aspect of business. That is why this Module is a must read for those building businesses. In start-up organizations, the financial impact of a bad hire can be crippling. Even if you do not fly someone in or put them in a hotel the cost is high. A clear, consistent and professional plan as well as regular reviews of these practices is extremely important to a company's success.

Module 6- Recruiting and Hiring
Lesson 6-8- Beware of Rainmakers

First, let's define "rainmakers". I have seen it defined as, "a person who brings in new business and wins new accounts almost by magic, since it is often not readily apparent how this new business activity is caused". Many companies in search of exponential growth will seek out folks that appear to be rainmakers. They believe that the person will attract more quality people and customers and thus replicate their past success.

I am sure some Rainmakers deliver what they promise, but in my experience they hardly ever do so. I have seen hundreds of thousands of dollars invested in these individuals. Rarely have I seen any return on these investments. This does not mean that they are not good at what they do. Nor does it mean they all overstate their success. I mean that this strategy is more often than not a loser. I feel that there are several reasons why it does not work. Some folks fall into multiple categories, but all fall into one of them.

- Sometimes their success was aided or caused by factors or situations that cannot or does not exist at the new company.
- The corporate structure and/or company dynamics that existed at their former place. For instance, the old company may have given this person a free rein to take dangerous risks. If they took one and it worked out, they were heroes. If the new company is risk averse, they may not be able to replicate previous successes.
- The timing of the innovation or strategy utilized before may no longer exist and thus will not work again.
- This person may have had a supporting cast that actually was responsible for the past success. Sometimes this person was not the real rainmaker. So, unless you hire the real rainmaker also, failure is probable.
- Sometimes the competitive culture at the previous place is not existent at the new one. Was the former company a known entity with immediate name recognition with prospective customers? Did this give them the foot in the door that often sets the process in motion? If your company does not have that name recognition, can this person be successful? Additionally, did the pricing at the old company get them the business? If so, their talent may not be as special as you think. If you are not able or willing to match the pricing, they probably will fail.

- Sometimes, the claims of success by the rainmaker are just plain B.S. I found this happening more often than not and more in today's world than in years past. I have to tell you, as someone that hired some possible rainmakers, phonies are not as easy as you may think to weed out. I have made several bad hires due to this situation. Even with, what I thought, was good due diligence, I have been fooled. As a leader this can ruin your company and your reputation. I often saw rainmakers that failed at my place find a new home with another company with a larger job elsewhere. Of course, they were out on their ear in six months or less, but unbelievably they surfaced soon in a larger role. And on and on. Amazing but true. You cannot do too much due diligence on rainmakers.

Before considering hiring a rainmaker you must look at each of the above factors to make sure they can bring you the success they had or appeared to have had at their previous employer. I would much rather grow my business organically from within. It carries less risk and motivates your current staff to stay and work hard.

Module 6- Recruiting and Hiring

Lesson 6-9- College recruits, the pros and cons

Hiring and training recent college graduates is a strategy that some companies have employed to add quality employees especially in a thin workforce environment. There are pros and cons to hiring these folks. There are also certain realities. I have found that it works best in a larger organization as it is a numbers game. That is due to the realities below;

- It requires a sizable investment in resources and absolute cost. You would normally pay the students during training. Initially they may provide little to no productivity. A dedicated teacher/coordinator will have to be assigned to the training.
- There will be immediate fallout of these folks once the training is complete. Training folks for work that they have never done without knowing that they will like the business is risky. They can complete the training and decide to leave because they are not interested in the field. I found that if we could get 6 or 7 out of 10 to make it through training and into production we were doing well.
- For the folks that make it through and begin working, you must realize that this is their first career job and most will not stick around forever. So, the turnover rate is greater than for the average experienced hire. Of the 6 or 7 that begin working, expect that 1 - 2 of them will leave after one year.
- Depending on the number of seats you need to fill, you could have two classes per year. (June graduates and December graduates).
- Because of the fallout you will need to repeat the training programs for years to come to keep your staffing correct.

So, why would you want to embark on a program to bring in and train new people?

- On one hand it is good to build your own workforce trained properly and thoroughly and come without bad habits or practices. Comprehensive training is the best way to learn as most people learn their trade in pieces. They learn a piece here and a piece there but it can take years to fill in the blanks in their knowledge base. Comprehensive training can provide a clear understanding of the big picture, the history of the business and how each role ties into the overall success.

- The young folks are like sponges and can learn quickly and are very adaptable. They can internalize concepts on the run. They, if motivated, have endless energy and many will have a thirst for knowledge that is conducive to this approach.
- In times where the workforce is depleted, it may be the only way to grow your staff.

Best Practices

- Find candidates within your organization first. There are always people hired for lower level work that prove to be prime candidates for development. This promotes high morale as people see a career path within your organization. These folks will provide a higher pull through percentage as compared to outsiders/recent graduates.
- The balance of your candidates will come from colleges. Find Deans of business at local universities and colleges. They are usually happy to assist you in identifying candidates that they would recommend.
- Select candidates first using the Job Fit personality tools mentioned in a previous lesson in this Module. Start by determining the correct dominant personality type for the job.
- Interview using the "rule of three" mentioned in a previous lesson in this Module.
- Have the students study half of the day and assist in your production teams the balance of the day. This will allow you to recoup some of the cost.
- Develop curriculum starting with industry jargon and acronyms. If you have manuals in your business you have a head start. However, these are usually too advanced for the newbies. They must be taught the basics and the concepts before learning their job.

I have introduced programs to develop young people with no experience through a training program like this. I will tell you that it helped my organization survive a period of time when business was growing geometrically and we simply ran out of trained people across the entire country. Once we understood the realities mentioned above, we really enjoyed the journey with these folks. Many of them are still in the business and thriving because they received a comprehensive training with all of the blanks filled in at the beginning of their career.

Module 7- Customer Focused Business

Lesson 7-1- The customer is not always right, but always important

For years customer service was a described to me as, "The customer is always right." I always had trouble with his concept. During High School I was working at a retail department store. Customers would come in and at times complain about the product or how they perceived the cost of an item based upon the signage. Often times they were absolutely wrong and I knew they were just trying to get away with something. My manager said to give it to them. Later she explained that the value of a returning customer was much higher than the loss on this one item. The customer is not always right but always important. What this quote really means is that the customer should feel that their point of view and the benefit of doing business is always important to their service provider. As such the service provider would do everything possible to accommodate them, their client. Most customers are reasonable people and just want what they paid for or expected.

So, when a customer calls with a problem sometimes they are right and the service provider is wrong. However, sometimes the client is not right, but misinformed, misled or just plain wrong in their accusation. Your job is to get to the bottom of their concern, clarify and give them the respect to have the issue reviewed. This is where the "important" idea comes into play. The service provider must then follow up and have it reviewed and get back to the client as soon as possible, but before it was promised. This is way too often not done. I mean following up with the client. They almost do not expect it. Many times, when they do receive a follow up call, even if it does not go their way, you have made a customer for life. You can stand out as a company or individual service provider by just doing what you promised. If the customer is misinformed you must inform. If they were misled you must assure them that the guilty party would be held accountable. If they are just being unreasonable you must do what you can to seek a middle ground to satisfy them. If that all fails and they are just unreasonable and long-term cheaters, do what I state in Lesson 7-7 of this Module and just fire them.

Module 7- Customer Focused Business

Lesson 7-2- Another Loan

I wrote and presented this piece some time ago to my sales and operations staff while I was managing a retail mortgage division. While it references a group of mortgage professionals, the thoughts and advice can easily translate to any service type organization. It can also be related to staff positions as your peers and employees are also people that you serve.

I was watching a medical TV show the other night. I was struck by the attitudes of the surgeons and their strong desire to compete for certain people's surgery. For the most part it was without even knowing anything about the patient. Their goals were to further their experience and be asked to take on even more difficult surgeries. They even referred to the surgery by the condition and not the name of the patient. I believe an amount of this attitude was a defense mechanism against becoming too emotionally involved in the patient because of the toll that must take when someone dies. However, the patient and their families were in a life and death situation. This illustrated to me how disconnected one can get when dealing with many cases in one day. It is certainly expedient to act in such a manner, but I feel something was wrong with this attitude.

The next day while I was dealing with some problem loans and realized that too often, we do the same thing. We forget that behind every mortgage application there are people and families.

Typically, there are;

Buyers and Sellers and their families

- They are involved in the single largest financial transaction of their life
- The uncertainty of whether or not this is a good decision
- They are often also selling their home and stressed over that transaction
- They have many stressful tasks to juggle to be ready to move into or out of their home. Things like moving vans, the kid's new school, etc.

Listing and Selling agents and their families

- Often times this is their only transaction for the month and hence their family's only paycheck. They have entrusted us with delivering on our promise to be professionals and care enough to do our best.

- They have in turn made promises to their clients that we will handle their transaction with care.
- There often are a string of other transactions tethered and dependent upon our service delivery.

Loan officers and other branch personnel and their families

1. This transaction may represent 50% or more of their family's income. Working on commission carries great financial opportunities but with it much stress as they have no salary.
2. They are relying upon the operations team from opening to post closing to recognize that families are reliant on their talents, professionalism, sense of urgency and focus on the closing date.

Operation team members and their families

1. Their employment is reliant on the sales force doing their job to originate, document, counsel, and proactively perform their duties in the process. Their shortcomings affect this loan but also delays other loans that may make the difference between our company's success or failure. Failure means losing their job.
2. Many are sole income providers for their families

In summary we must avoid the tendency to look at the transaction as another loan. There are many real people and their children relying on our care, understanding and sense of urgency. We must care enough to know our job and proactively serve our customers both internally and externally. There are faces and lives behind every loan.

Rob Cosentino SVP, National Production Executive

Module 7- Customer Focused Business

Lesson 7-3- Managing customer expectations

Better to promise a result a day longer than expected than to deliver a minute late. This is an interesting human nature reality. This is best described with two anecdotes;

1. In dealing with an irate customer, I made a promise to get back with them by 4PM that day. I was caught in traffic (in the days before cellphones) and did not get back until 4:05PM. They called and left a message at 4:03PM that they were disappointed that I lied to them.
2. A borrower was wanting a timeframe for the completion of an appraisal on their new home. I knew that it is typically back in one week, ten days at worst. I told them two weeks. They were not thrilled with the timeframe, but after I explained how busy they were, the customer understood. The appraisal was back in one week and the borrower was surprised and very happy.

Communication is the key to keeping customers happy. What I should have done in case 1 was to call them before I got in the car and told them I may be a couple minutes late. That is managing expectations. I probably would ask them If I could get back to them as late as 4:30. Then when I got back to them at 4:05PM, they would have had a good surprise. You must be painfully clear to people what to expect. You must also re-state it several times and in writing if possible. I would sometimes, with particularly challenging customers, ask them to repeat what I promised them so that I knew they got it. Verbalizing it makes it difficult for them to forget or dispute.

Another aspect has to do with delivering bad news. No matter how bad it is, you must relay the information as soon as possible. That is either right away or after you try to clarify the issue and sometimes find another option. But never overnight.

If you are in a service business, delivering service IS your business. Clearly communicating what the customer can expect from you and always delivering is the best marketing strategy. When someone says to me that this company always kept them informed and was honest with them, even when problems arose, I will consider using them myself.

On a topic relating to this subject I will add the following few thoughts;

The main job of any organization is to create and keep customers. No matter how wonderful your product or service is, an inability to create and keep customers will doom your company. I am providing many customer related tips in this lesson and other sections of this book. Below are a couple others that seems appropriate to add here.

Always earn their business- never take them or their business for granted. Your eagerness, and the relentless pursuit of their business must be evident to every customer or they will eventually leave you. Nobody wants to feel that they are being taken for granted. You must not lose touch with your good clients while prospecting for more. The tactics used to accomplish this need not be grandiose or expensive. It can be as simple as an informal call from the owner to the customer. Of course, showing your appreciation could include things of value. The fact that you are thinking of them is powerful. This is especially true when you have grown your business since the beginning of the relationship. If they feel that you do not forget the relationships that help you to be successful, they are less likely to become jealous of your success or seek another supplier or partner.

Measure your performance and brag about it- you should constantly be measuring your success in the areas of profits, service delivery and growth. Monitoring these things at all times makes sure you see trends, both positive and negative, early and before others notice. This information should always be handled promptly and seriously. When the news is good do not be afraid to share it with others. Let your customers know the good news and thank them for their hand in your success. As your customers are also your employees do the same with them. Bragging is good when humility is shown simultaneously.

Module 7- Customer Focused Business
Lesson 7-4- Live in their shoes

One of the best instinctive qualities that I possess is the ability to "live in other's shoes". Simply put it is the ability to look at a situation from another person's perspective. To see it as they see it. To understand "where they are coming from". This ability can serve you well in many aspects of business and life. If you cannot or will not try to live in other's shoes, your life will be more difficult than it otherwise would or should be. Part of this includes having empathy for the other person's plight.

I will focus on just four applications for this ability;

1. Negotiating business deals/sales
2. Managing people- what motivates them
3. Meeting customer's needs
4. Raising children

Negotiating business deals/sales- I have used a technique when dealing with business transactions and in sales situations. I will give you an example of the latter. When I was selling real estate, I would almost always be involved in the negotiations of the terms and conditions of the sales contract. While I never had the buyer and seller in the same room, I would make it my business to learn the (1) point of view, (2) important needs and (3) motivation of each side. Often times, if, for instance, I was representing the buyer, I would have the opportunity to meet with the sellers directly. Sometimes I would have to go through the other Realtor. In any case, I would dig for the three points mentioned above. How do you do this? Simply, ask questions relating to the three topics and shut up and listen. Keep questioning until you reveal the answer to each of the questions. I would have already done so for my clients, the buyers. Now I am armed with the tools to negotiate with both, knowing what their hot buttons are, etc. As I speak to each party, I keep in mind the perspective of each side and try to find common ground and solutions to meet them.

Managing people- Dealing with employees, either to resolve issues, understand their problems or find out what motivates them, I would use similar tactics. For instance, if there was a dispute between individuals, I would first seek to understand how each of them sees the issue, the result they are seeking and the most important win they must have to be satisfied. My questions to each would be directed to those ends. With this arsenal of information, I can get in the middle and negotiate a solution. I can only do this if I live in their shoes.

Meeting customer's needs- In order to meet customer's needs you must know how it feels to be your customer. How they are treated, how easy it is to communicate, how good the product or service is and your reputation to care. You must "live in their shoes". If it is possible, the best way is to act as a customer. This would give you firsthand information. Call into customer service and see how you and your issue is treated. Alternatively reaching out to your customers and question them on the specific aspect of their needs. Keep asking until you understand and ask many customers. Surveys are helpful in these matters for a general understanding, but direct contact is always needed.

Raising children- Understanding where your child is coming from is very difficult. It takes much trust and open communications. Like every other aspect of parenting you cannot wait until they are 12 or 15 years old to begin building trust and communication. But if you do this, living in their shoes is an invaluable tool to gain understanding and provide proper guidance to your child.

If you are not a natural at living in other's shoes, you have some work to do to understand the strategy. The most important thing to understand is it all starts with communications and specifically deep listening.

Module 7- Customer Focused Business
Lesson 7-5- Handling Irate Customers.

"The nearly fool proof technique"

As a manager or owner of a business you will be required to handle irate customers. Many times, your subordinates will handle many of them, but the real difficult ones come to you. Much of the time it is more about how they were treated than receiving the goods or services you are providing. But past that anger there is always the fulfillment of the delivery of the goods or services that really matter to them. I will use a mortgage related example.

The Customer is trying to get approved and close on a mortgage to purchase a home. There has been delays in getting their approval and they feel the processor is unresponsive and not getting the job done. They are very angry at the attitude of the individual and cannot understand why they are being treated in this way. During the conversation they state that a deadline to get approved is near and they could lose the home if not approved in time.

Step 1- Let them talk and get everything off their chest. Do not interrupt and do not defend. Many times, just dumping their anger on you calms them down if they feel you are listening.

Step 2- Separate the poor service from the task at hand. Apologize for the bad experience and assure them that you will get to the bottom of this.

Step 3- "The Technique"- Tell them that while you work on the customer service issue let's get the most important thing done. In this case, get them approved. Tell them that you will make this happen and then do it, now. The magic is that in 95% of the cases, once you deliver on the approval, they forget about the service issue. However, certainly follow up with them on this, but usually they say that it was not that big of a deal.

Module 7- Customer Focused Business
Lesson 7-6- Fulfill their needs and you do not have to sell

I am often asked, "What is the key to making a successful sale?" I guess they are looking for that magic sauce, that miracle technique that makes people buy. Certainly, there are strategies and techniques that can be effective. There are some terrific strategies that I have used over the years and I have chronicled them in this book. However, all strategies and successful sales come as a result of doing one thing.

So, here is the "MAGIC".

If you can fulfill the customer's needs you will make the sale.
What do I mean? If a customer needs a result, a resource, a product or service and you can provide it to them, then they sell themselves on the item. No hard sell or aggressive techniques will help if you do not fulfill their needs. Of course, your product must be at a fair price, be of quality and be efficiently delivered. Your first job is to find out what the customers need. That is often not as simple as deciding that they need the item. Many times, you will be much more successful if you understand what the motivation for the need might be. Is this part of an overall strategy to forward the customer's agenda? Understanding this will allow you to tailor the sales presentation, indeed the strategy, to hone in directly on their hot buttons.

Sometimes they do not know how much they need the item and sometimes they do not even know they need it. This part goes to the sales techniques themselves. Many books have been written on the subject of developing a realization for the customer that they really need what you are selling. Once they are convinced that they need your product or service, you are 75% home. Neil Rackham wrote a book that was published in 1988, "Spin Selling". This is a tremendous book teaching a strategy that I have used for many years. I highly recommend getting a copy and reading it. The concept, in an over-simplified form, is to know their needs and how they relate to what your selling and then develop a series of questions that, when answered by the customer, basically moves them to telling you that they need your product or service. Once they believe they need it you are done. You also see examples of a way to create the need for the product or service even when one is not there. This works mostly for impulse buying as often the urgency of the purchase is exaggerated. I am speaking of "Infomercials". Yes, these forms of sales techniques are extremely successful. They convince you in a few minutes that your life will change if you buy this mop. They show many instances of miracle results and this builds a sense of need. Then they add to the offer many other options and say you can only get all of this if you call in the next 30 minutes. Thus, a sense of urgency is created and you are buying 25 CD's at 2 o'clock in the morning. Having a strategy to develop a sense of need and urgency can be very powerful. But for normal sales just understanding and meeting the customer's needs is the key to success in sales.

Module 7- Customer Focused Business

Lesson 7-7- Addition by Subtraction

Many customer relationships are good and positive. Everyone does their thing and we all make money. There are however, those type of relationships that are harmful to you and/or your business. They are usually one sided in the benefits and that is never good. If left unchecked, they can undermine personal relationships, a business strategy or a company in general. I am referring to bad relationships. More specifically I mean "toxic" relationships. Often times you are not sure how or when the relationship turned sour. I will only focus here on the business type of bad relationship. These can either be a situation with an employee or a customer. I spend time in a later lesson discussing the toxic employee (see Module 9, Lesson 9-2 "Cancer in the Organization"). Here I will focus upon customer relationships.

I have found that there are two situations from which most toxic business relationships occur. 1) doing business with friends or family or, 2) A very large client that means a great deal to the bottom line or your standing in the business community. You will put up with a lot more hassle from these two customers as there is a perceived consequence. There have been times when I realized that I was spending more time with one of these customers than all of my other customers combined. Certainly, there are times when this is necessary. If there is an occasional relationship threatening situation going on it is prudent to spend more time with them. That is common sense and part of business. However, some relationships are, in the final analysis, toxic. This is an easy predicament to fall into. The customer calls you every day and complains. You stay in a constant scenario of crisis. So, you spend more time thinking of the situation and dealing with the issue of the day. In the case of a toxic relationship, there is constantly a life-threatening situation and the customer constantly threatens to leave you if you do not handle it now and usually at the financial or moral detriment to you and/or your company. You are always on the defensive. It is vital that you address the problem.

Firstly, try to reason with the counterparty and explain how you feel and see if there is an amicable solution. Solving this is a win-win situation. The client may be unaware of what you are going through. If that does not work or they retreat to the same old tactics another tactic is required. In its extreme, some relationships smother your ability to grow your business and service your other existing clients.

When the demand for your time continues beyond the crisis or there are threats that you must continue to devote this level of focus to maintain the relationship, you must reevaluate the relationship. You should realize that there are relationships that you simply cannot afford to keep. You should always consider moving away from these toxic relationships. That is what I call addition by subtraction. When you move away from the bad relationship and spend your now, free time to focus on old clients and add to your client base, it is amazing how much time you will free up and how liberating it becomes.

However, it is not wise to make this move before evaluating the impact. You should endure the heat and keep the cash flow coming while you plan to replace and rebuild. You may indeed be in a situation that losing the client would result in cash flow issues and revenue loss that you cannot survive. This brings us to the theory that you should never allow one relationship to represent such a significant percentage of your revenue that losing it would be catastrophic. That does not mean to say that this situation may not occur in the short term. It means that if it does, you should be making plans to add to your client base to bring that level of dependency on the large client to an acceptable level. By the way, you will be growing your business as well.

Bottom line is that even if firing your toxic customer hurts financially in the short term, it is always a winner for you. My advice is to recognize it early, make sure that you are not relying on one customer to make your company successful, plan your move and get rid of them.

If you find yourself in this situation, make plans for addition by subtraction.

Module 8- People Management
Lesson 8-1- What motivates people

One of the most important jobs of an organization is to understand what will motivate its employees to perform their tasks at a high level while they achieve personal and professional satisfaction. At some level, you are motivated to keep at it when it is not fun or not easy or not profitable. Whether it is a sense of personal achievement, pride in helping others or something for which you have a natural talent, you must be motivated.

The single most important concept is that everyone is not motivated by the same thing. So, what motivates people? Ken Blanchard says "what motivates people is what motivates people" Your motivation is fed by your highest level of need that you have not yet attained. When you are homeless you are motivated by having a place to sleep. A millionaire is not motivated by having a home as they may have many of those. I urge you to "Google" Maslow's Hierarchy of Needs. Link is below. I not only believe in this theory but have used it in managing people including my children for many years. It presents a pyramid of the following needs:

Lowest

- Food and Shelter
- Safety, Health, Security
- Sense of Belonging
- Esteem/Recognition
- Self-Actualization

Highest

To understand what motivates an individual you must first understand where they are on the hierarchy of needs. For instance, a person who is homeless is at the lowest end of the scale. They are singularly focused upon finding food and a place to sleep. They will be motivated to perform the most difficult even demeaning tasks to satisfy this most basic need.

Before we go any further there are three concepts, we must understand to utilize the strategy.

People can move through various levels towards satisfying that next need. So, motivating them can be a moving target. Sometimes it is as simple as more money or more inclusion into another layer of management.

A person cannot be motivated by something that either helps them achieve a need they have already achieved or is beyond their current level of need. A person may not be willing or motivated to do something that will motivate a homeless person looking for their next meal. Conversely a person in need of money to support their family will not be motivated by a recognition plaque unless it is also tied to a bonus or raise.

People can fulfill needs outside of the workplace. These people may never be motivated to a higher level from their work environment. People may be happy meeting their financial needs at work and find their higher levels satisfied elsewhere. For instance, one could fill their need for sense of belonging through a charitable endeavor. They perceive their job as a means to an end to provide their financial needs. These are your solid and valuable low to mid-level managers. They do their job and do it well. They are generally self-motivated to put their time in and retire with benefits.

While a person cannot suddenly achieve all levels of need above them, the can certainly and instantly drop from a very high level down to the most basic need. This sudden change happens when someone loses their job, experiences a tragedy or becomes seriously ill. I witnessed a most precipitous drop in level of need when in August of 1992, Hurricane Andrew devastated parts of South Florida. Two days after the storm I joined a group to provide relief for these victims. We found our way to what was once a rather affluent area of South Miami where many business executives lived. Most of the homes were either completely destroyed or at least unlivable. Their personal effects were often gone. The roads in and out were mostly impassable and their vehicles were mostly destroyed or inaccessible. Adding to the tragedy there was no electricity or phone service. We set up a location to distribute food, water and ice for these folks. Their faces revealed their shock and disorientation. These were folks that for the most part had achieved the higher levels of need, beautiful home, financially secure, highly regarded in their community and workplace now suddenly and dramatically dropped down the hierarchy of needs to the most basic need for food and shelter. This happened in one night. They had no access to money and nowhere to spend it if they had some. They were seeking food, ice and a place for their family to sleep.

When relating this to the workplace, most people we hire below a senior management level are either in need of the Safety and Security level or Sense of Belonging level.

So, let's first examine individuals who have achieved the food and shelter need but is seeking safety health and security. What motivates these folks is money and/or employment benefits. They have a place to live but need the financial resources to care for themselves and families. A majority of the workforce falls into this level. Working folks trying to make ends meet all the way up to people looking to accumulate the necessary wealth to provide more options for themselves and family. These folks can begin to be motivated by the next level of need (sense of belonging) and also be motivated by money. Just to be clear, most folks always are motivated by money, even if they have plenty. But other things can motivate them more as they move up the hierarchy of needs.

The sense of belonging is what transforms a drudgery of job into a place to which they enjoy coming every day. The sense of community that many find at work often results in friendships outside of the workplace. These folks are motivated by being appointed to committees, project teams, etc. They still want to make more money, but these other things are non-monetary motivators. These are the folks that say they love their job. Many times, it is not their work but their sense of community that they love. Groups of these individuals often are gathered in the most effective teams inside any organization.

Next is the need for self-esteem and recognition. People seeking this level are highly motivated by awards, winning contests for performance and award trips for top producers. They enjoy the actual award, but they are driven by the need to be recognized as the best. A person whose opinion is sought. These are your sales and service leaders. I once managed a woman who was a very good sales person as a loan originator. However, she was the leading salesperson in the nation selling life insurance to her borrowers. She made much more money originating loans than she did selling the insurance. It was actually pennies. However, she was motivated by the annual awards trip and the recognition she received by being the best. Her income was good enough, but the recognition motivated her. These folks are also your junior and senior level managers who are motivated by the title and breadth of management scope. These folks may be happy with a larger title even if it may not carry additional income.

Reaching self-actualization is rare and is cherished. This level exists when what you do is hard to distinguish from who you are. It is no longer clear where work ends and living your life begins. These can be first responders, social workers, teachers, health care providers, clergy, corporate leaders and others. The most graphic example can be a clergyman, especially priests. They are singularly called to this life and become what they do. You may not ever reach this level; however, you should find a career/business that will continue to motivate you through all of the levels you have yet to reach.

The concept of a "calling" brings me to an observation I have made from my years on this earth. There are individuals among us who are specially called or find a calling in what starts out as a job. Some of these are teachers, police, firefighters, military, clergy, social workers, healthcare workers like nurses, etc. To their financial detriment they are so motivated by their calling that satisfies their needs for self-esteem, recognition and often self-actualization that they settle for lower financial rewards. Our institutions, in my opinion, have taken advantage of this fact and have paid them less than the value of their service. This has been tolerated because these folks are so driven that they make the sacrifice. Shame on us as a nation. Okay, off my soapbox.

To summarize this lesson, motivating people will be different for each person. Most of this will be based upon the next level in the Hierarchy of needs they have yet to achieve. Knowing how to motivate people can be an invaluable tool in your arsenal to help your company achieve higher and higher goals.

https://en.wikipedia.org/wiki/Maslow%27s_hierarchy_of_needs#Esteem

Module 8- People Management
Lesson 8-2- Managing Up

There are many books providing guidance on managing people. They focus mainly on managing people who work for you directly or indirectly. Managing in general is a combination of acting as a leader and facilitator. Much of the time you are teaching, decision making, evaluating people, plans and the business environment.

What most books do not teach you is managing up. What do I mean by managing up? Managing up is providing support, direction, evaluations on people, plans and the business environment to your superior(s). Being able to manage up can make you an essential team member and further your career. You can manage up for various reasons.

- Help shape and form the opinion of your superior on a given topic to further the growth and health of the organization
- To fill in possible gaps in your manager's talents, knowledge base on factors important for his or her decision-making role
- Enhance the image of your superior inside and outside of the organization

I spent much time in my career doing this and it was one of the primary factors that led to my personal success. This role can be very good to your career or it can end it. By this I mean you can do it well or do it poorly. To do it well the following principles/imperatives must guide you

1. Do everything with a "pure heart". This means nothing should be done that is not in the best interest of your superior and the company. Personal gain should not play a role in what you do or say. And never let personal feelings for others play any role in your actions. If that ever happens, the trust will be broken and your career with your superior is over.
2. Know your stuff. Make sure you thoroughly research the issue or idea before presenting. Understand the pros and cons and possible unintended consequences.
3. Do not provide any managing up initiatives with an audience. Do this in private to not embarrass your superior.
4. You must always be truthful with your superior, but you must be mindful of the personality of your superior. Some will appreciate brutal honesty and want you to tell the them if "they screwed up". Others may have a personality that requires a subtler approach.

5. Do it in a manner to not demean your superior. Instead of telling him/her that she is lacking or uninformed, describe how you or others do or understand an issue.

All of this, if done with the above in mind, will help develop a mutual trust between you and your superior that provides him/her a teammate that makes them a better manager/leader. Additionally, you will be viewed as a vital supporter and you will be top of mind for opportunities for your personal growth.

Module 8- People Management

Lesson 8-3- Manage everyone the same and you lose

People come into your life/business world possessing various type of personalities. They have many different goals, levels of talent, motivations and expectations. They come from all different cultural environments, family histories and religious beliefs. That is why I am puzzled why so many books on managing people use a cookie cutter, one size fits all approach. There is no way you can manage everyone the same way with the same plan. The job of a managing among other things is to recruit and select, coach, mentor and motivate your people. Given the myriad combinations of the above differences between people, how could you approach the management of everyone the same? There are many books on people management and I urge you to read as many as you can. My syllabus at the end of this book contains some of these. This does not suggest that you treat people differently for any reasons of race, creed or sexual preference. I mean that how you approach the management of people should be tailored to the person so that you have the best chance of helping them succeed, learn and grow.

A second thought is how you handle truly gifted superstar level talents within your organization. A purist would suggest that you treat everyone the same. I am reminded of a line contributed to Jimmy Johnson, legendary football coach at the University of Miami and the Dallas Cowboys. He was one of just three coaches ever to win a National Collegiate Championship and a Super Bowl. When someone accused him of treating his superstar athlete differently than others he said,

*"People have misconstrued my treating players differently. Same offense, good player disciplined, so-so player cut! All players disciplined."

While he disciplined everyone for offenses, the penalty or consequences will not be the same. Talent is rare.

In summary you must find methods of management that have the best chance to make the person the employee they can be. Make your intentions crystal clear and over-communicate your management plan. You must be consistent. Jimmy Johnson was consistent in his own way. Make sure you are too.

* https://cowboyszone.com/threads/jimmy-johnson-on-disciplining-players.358538/

Module 8- People Management

Lesson 8-4- Separation Interview should not last more than five minutes

As a young manager of an operations group I was facing a daunting challenge. The company was mired in a major financial crisis. Entire divisions the size of most corporations was in danger of closing down. These were difficult times. It was determined that a layoff would occur on a specific morning. Only senior managers were aware it was going to happen to our division. I, like many of my peers, had a number of people to terminate on that day. This was particularly disturbing as we had let people go a couple of months back. The difference here was that we already had moved out the bottom 20% of the group. The lower performers were gone and only really good people remained and I had to let nine of them go. We were told of the schedule several days in advance. I have always found that the time between becoming aware of bad news and the time we were allowed to share the news with my people is gut wrenching. Facing them every day when they do not know what was coming was very difficult. Looking back after many years and after I have had to shut down entire divisions, this seems to be a small number. But it was my first layoff of this size. I did not sleep very well during that week leading up to D-Day.

My previous experience terminating one person here or there was difficult as you are affecting a person's life. Too often the discussion blossomed into a full-blown lengthy discourse with much emotion and reflection. While it seemed humane to commiserate with the person, I saw that it did not help them in the long run and did not change their view of my decision or their actions that led to the termination. Sometime things were said in anger that were embarrassing to the individual. In subsequent years a very good policy mandates an exit interview after termination. This is done some time (days) after the termination and handled by a different party, usually an HR professional. Once much of the initial shock and emotions have passed, a more constructive discussion can be had. This interview not only reinforces the company's position but allows the former employee to air any complaints about working conditions, policies or individuals they feel need to be addressed. Bad actors within a company can be identified when people can speak without risk of job loss as a retaliation. Management should monitor the results of these meetings to determine if problems exist within the company.

Getting back to my layoff situation, as I said, I was really struggling with the task. While we were given guidance in the steps in the process, where to send the people afterward and such, no guidance was given as to the nature of the discussion itself. I spoke to some more experienced peers and they gave me a few pointers. But nothing was offered that made me feel any better. The day before the layoff was to occur, I went to my boss. I did this in a bit of desperation as my boss, while a good person, was not a very good communicator and seemed a bit cold to other's feelings. While he was always honest when you asked him a direct question, he rarely offered any information. I once found out about a raise I received only when I saw a difference in my paycheck. I went to ask if this was a mistake and he said that he forgot to let me know. But I was at wit's end about these impending layoffs and asked to see him. I told him that I was really struggling with this upcoming layoff and why. He said he understood my feeling but knew that it was normal for anyone with some compassion. I mentioned that I was always uncomfortable with the conversations with people being terminated. It was gut wrenching and the thought of going through this emotional roller coaster nine times was scary. I asked him if he had any techniques that could make it any better for the person and myself. He asked me what approach I was planning. I explained that I would tell them what was going on, indicate my deep regret, ask them their feelings, discuss their plans and listen to their concerns. I would allow at least thirty minutes to spend with each employee to fully go through the steps. He then gave me advice that was totally unexpected. He told me to conduct the meeting as follows;

1. Greet the person and immediately explain that there was a layoff happening and, unfortunately, they were one of the people being affected.
2. Tell them that their severance and benefits would be explained by HR in the next room.
3. Thank them for their work, stand up and lead them out the door
4. The meeting should be less than 5 minutes
5. Do not commiserate, just discuss facts and move on.

Less than five minutes? I was stunned. How could this guy suggest such a cold approach to this traumatic experience? Are people so insignificant that he would just pull the rug from under them and walk away? I was never shy with anyone when I felt something must be said. Even with superiors. I collected myself and said, "that is the coldest approach I have ever heard. It was cruel and makes it look like you did not care about their plight." My boss sat back in his chair and asked me how well, my approach worked. I admitted that it was very traumatic for the person and sometimes things get nasty. He said that in his experience, the long-term effect of that approach caused some bad feelings and generally the discussions did not help the employee. Many were embarrassed that another person witnessed their high emotions resulting from the shock. He explained that it was much like pulling off a bandage. If you pull it off slowly, it is much more painful. He offered that this approach cannot make the experience good, but this one usually does not make things any worse long term. I told him that I would like to think about this. So, I left his office and started thinking about what he had said. I, selfishly liked the idea of a quick meeting. I realized that my current approach did not really make it better for the person. My boss had been around for a long time and I figured I would give it a try on at least the first meeting.

The next morning, after not much sleep, I set up the first meeting. I held my breath and conducted the meeting as my boss had instructed. When it was over, I at least knew that it was no worse than my approach and the person's dignity remained intact. I did it for all nine meetings. Once I had met with all the affected people, I went back to my boss's office and told him that while it was a tough experience, I felt that it was much better than my old way. In the next few weeks, I heard from some of the people who actually thanked me for the professional way I handled the meeting.

From that time forward, I used this approach and think of my old boss each time I pull off a bandage.

Module 8- People Management

Lesson 8-5-Being fired should never be a surprise

The most important business practice and life practice for that matter is open and honest communications. Opportunities lost and hardships follow poor communications. When people are up front and communicate regularly and with a pure heart, life is much easier. Maybe not easy but definitely easier. You must never assume that another person sees things as you do. Nor do they have the same expectations as you do. Because of this people must talk freely. You may find different perceptions exist or hidden issues are under the surface. Talking about them may not be easy but it is vital to a healthy relationship.

In the context of a business environment it is vital for company health. Misconceptions can lead to disharmony within a work environment. Employees are owed regular communications about company plans, direction and results. I believe in frequent company meetings to communicate these things and also allow the free flow of thoughts and concerns to and from the staff.

When it comes to managing people, this concept is paramount. If open and regular feedback is not given to an employee how do they know they are doing well? How do they know they are not? The communications do not always have to be formal. Sometimes a simple correction can be done on the fly. That being said, it is of utmost importance to have a formalized performance review process within all organizations. It can be monthly, quarterly, semi-annually or annually. They can also be at any time a serious breach is suspected in performance or attitude. This process should include a clear assessment of performance from various perspectives. They can be objective and subjective. Usually some of both is required. This review must also include corrective measures for improvement with definitive means of measurement. It should also include goals for the next period of time. If there are deficiencies in performance, the employee should be aware of what the expected results should be to improve performance. They must also know the consequences or next steps to expect if performance is not improved. They should be given the opportunity to respond to the review and provide their commentary of their situation and the company in general.

This practice is not only fair to the employee as they know what to expect and where they stand but protects the company legally as you document discussions and direction. So, if you need to terminate someone you can show the basis for the termination and how the shortcomings were explained to the employee. The practice can help you develop employees into better versions of themselves. You can help them grow professionally and change the things they need to change so as to contribute better to the bottom line of the company. Too many good people are lost when they are not afforded the respect of good, clear communications.

I have often found that this practice makes it easier to manage. When someone has been managed properly, they know well in advance that they are not meeting expectations. When they feel they cannot meet them they often quit before you even have to fire them. This is a much better result than having to let them go. Even when you do have to release someone, it should never be a surprise if you have had regular corrective action communications. If they are surprised you have not done your job.

In summary, regular and fair reviews of your people is not only a good business practice but it is the right thing to do for the individuals.

Module 8- People Management

Lesson 8-6- Catch people doing good things but no Participation Certificates

A good manager/executive pays close attention and stays as close as possible to the people on the ground doing the company's business. As discussed in the previous lesson, this goes a long way to developing good morale and improves retention.

As mentioned in an earlier lesson, one of the six levels of needs according to Maslow* is the need for "esteem". All humans have a need to be respected. Many of your employees are very motivated by being shown respect and appreciation. Motivating your people is a primary requirement for a healthy organization. Satisfying their next level of need is motivating in itself. While you are walking around or monitoring the troops you should take every opportunity to catch people doing things in an extraordinary manner. I am not referring to just doing their job but going the extra mile exerting significantly more effort than what is expected. It does not have to be a large thing but it must be above and beyond. The recognition can be as minimal as a "Way to Go" or more including company-wide recognition. In larger organizations we have had regular recognition programs. The rewarded efforts should be doing those things that support the mission statement of the company and/or helps the company meet its long and short- term goals. Be careful not to minimize the value of this recognition by using a low standard for the reward.

As I stated above there is a big difference between somebody consistently doing what is expected, showing up every day, doing their daily quota of activity or results and someone who exerts extraordinary effort or caring. The former group of people are vital to your business and usually make up a majority of the staff. Make sure they know they are appreciated. They should receive regular salary increases and be encouraged to learn and do more to be promoted in the organization. The latter should be rewarded and/or recognized. What I am not a fan of in any form is special recognition for just doing their job. In today's world we have grown accustomed to the practice of giving out "Participation Certificates". Our children are being given the wrong view of the real world. Showing up and doing your job is admirable but it is not worthy of special recognition. Participating is not special it is the minimum required. We should not minimize "exceptionalism" by rewarding folks for showing up.

Module 8- People Management

Lesson 8-7- Never fly at 30,000 feet

I have witnessed and mentored under people with a wide array of management styles. I have also seen people fail and exceed as managers. One interesting thing is that I have seen two people use the same style and one be very effective and the other fail as a manager. Many books are written on styles so I will not attempt to rewrite their fine work. I will, however, provide a few observations on managing in some specific situations.

In larger organization it is way too common for upper management to make decisions in a vacuum. This phenomenon happens when the management believes that they know what is happening on the street without checking. I call this "flying at 30,000 feet". Sometimes they talked to the field a while ago and believe it is still as they knew it or saw it then. Other times, they have one or two people they talk to on the ground and believe that they are the entire experience of the rank and file. It is most prevalent in organizations with multiple layers of managers managing managers. The result is upper management getting in a room and making changes to policies, procedures or strategies that are so out of touch with the street that they appear foolish or worse uncaring. Earning the respect of every employee is one of the most important jobs of upper management. It is just as important that the employees feel that they are respected by upper management. The latter comes from the employees witnessing management taking the time to talk to them, live in their shoes for a while and really listening to them in a meaningful way. Gathering small groups in an informal setting and becoming comfortable with each other to share their thoughts and concerns is required. You should be honest with them and tell them that you will not do everything they ask as other factors may preclude implementation. But listen and following through goes a long way. There are many other ways to immerse yourself on the street level. Do this regularly and your decisions will be made for the right reasons with all of the information at your fingertips.

There is a specific challenge in organizations that grow very fast and more layers of management are added between the upper management and the line folks. It is a similar challenge when you are promoted above your former peers. When either of the above happens a natural separation of daily interactions occur. You may not have time to go see the folks as your new duties forces you to focus on the big picture concerns. As time goes on you can get caught up in your own world and forget to stay in touch with those people you spent all your time with a while back. This problem slapped me straight in the face early in my career. I was fortunate enough to have been promoted twice in a year and a half. From working with the sales people, I was now managing the entire sales and operations group. There were two managers between me and those sales folks I started with. I was busy and felt that I was still respected by them and I certainly thought the world of each of them. The new responsibilities were quite daunting and I felt stressed at the challenge. One day I was walking down the hall and someone grabbed my arm. It was Sandy, a loan officer I started with when I started. She was a very good sales person and more importantly someone I looked upon as a friend. She was not a shy person and would always tell you what she was thinking. She pulled me into an empty office. She said, "did I do something to upset you?" I told her that she certainly did not. She said then why, when you walk down the hall and I am coming the other way, do you ignore me and do not even say hello. I was in disbelief and said, "I certainly never did that." She said, "Rob, you have been doing that for several months." I was late for a meeting so I told her that I would speak to her in the morning. That night I was deeply disturbed by this encounter. I really liked Sandy and thought the world of her. Why would she say such a thing? I began to reflect upon my demeanor and the amount of focus that was required to handle this new job. The next morning, I called her into my office. I asked her again if I was really doing that to her and she confirmed it. She said I looked straight ahead and did not even acknowledge her. It hit me that I was so focused upon my challenges that I was not paying attention to the present. I begged her to forgive me and then I thanked her for grabbing and straightening me out. From that day forward, I made sure that when I was walking around, I looked at those around me and always greeted them, especially Sandy.

I carried that moment with me forward throughout the next 30+ years. As an example, when I was managing a 100+ person operations center, I would take 30-45 minutes every morning I could and walked up and down through all of the cubicles and just said hello. It became so important to them that I would take the time that when I missed a few days, they let me hear it the next time. I had a bond with those folks that transcended normal business relationships. We always kept it professional, but it was more informal. They would do anything for me. This also gave me ground floor intelligence on what was going on in the teams. This was very important to my success. I was very happy during those times and continued the practice throughout my career even when they were in different cities. I would get out of the office and see them regularly. Later, I read an article that defined this practice as "Managing by Walking Around." After that talk with Sandy, I realized that it was actually my natural style. I never forgot my beginnings. I never forgot not having much and being at the bottom of the organization chart. I was the same person when I was at the top. I always knew that these are good and real people with goals and ambitions. They deserved my respect. I believe this is why today, after my retirement, I get calls and well wishes from people I worked with years ago.

Module 8- People Management
Lesson 8-8- Coaching Sales to create Referrals

"If you have not worked on your Referral Base today you are not finished working!"

Rob Cosentino

Our lifeblood in business is our referrals. Whether you are a sales person or business owner, without them we do not succeed. They sustain us, they complement our income and they are the cheapest marketing channel in the world, FREE.

So, every day you should be doing at least one activity to either create or keep referrals.

Creating Referrals- You can earn a referral, market for a referral or just ask for one. You earn a referral by doing the very best job you can for your client. Being professional is an overused word, but to me it means being knowledgeable, attentive, honest and always displaying a superior work ethic. Every phone call, every appointment and meeting are your opportunity to earn referrals. Marketing for referrals is vital as it creates customers that may not be naturally motivated to refer your business to others. It should be a regularly scheduled task on your calendar. Asking for a referral can be a simple as wearing a name tag while shopping. It can be engaging someone in your normal course of private life. You never know where or when a referral opportunity exists.

Keeping Referrals- Staying in touch with your referral base on a personal level is as important as creating them. If you create and not work to keep them, you will never achieve your personal goals. It is the easiest and most productive of these activities. Take time each day to contact a number of referral sources.

Each of these activities can be done using any media. You can make phone calls, send fliers, etc. The electronic opportunities are endless from email to texting to blogging and beyond. Social media is another tool to ask for referrals. These activities take much less time than they did just a few years ago. So not having the time is not an excuse and a recipe for mediocrity. I do caution not to rely on social media exclusively as everyone in the world markets online and the field is over-saturated.

So, every day perform some of these activities and one day your referrals will be the bulk of your business and your earnings potential will rise exponentially.

Module 9- Working Environment

Lesson 9-1- Organizational structure must make business sense

Setting your business up with the appropriate structure can make or break the venture. The necessary structure will change over time. You must be sure you have the proper balance of necessary resources to meet your current needs and at the same time avoiding too many hands in the pot. Let's start by looking at the two extreme ends of the challenge.

For smaller businesses, especially with a leader with special hands on experience and/or talents, the risk is having too little help. If there is one common challenge in a business like this it is the owner not being willing to delegate responsibilities. There is often a reticence to even hire help. The only way a business can grow exponentially is to have enough hands to complete the amount of work required for the next level of success. Let me give an illustration. Say you have a cabinet making business. You are the person designing and building the cabinets and have a helper. Business is good and you are working day and night to keep up. You know that your business not only requires the master cabinet maker but needs someone marketing, negotiating and selling the work. You need bookkeeping, government filings, and payroll to be done. You need to purchase the lumber, hardware and tools. You are very good at all of this. Then you realize you are at capacity in the amount of cabinets you can sell and deliver within reasonable timeframes. Most owners will not be willing to delegate any of this to others as, "nobody can do it as well as me". It may be true that you may not find anyone better than you at anything you do. But what are your alternatives? If you are content with the volume of business and the resultant income, continue on. If not, something must change. You could start out by finding someone to do the activities not directly relating to cabinet making. That may give you more time to build quality cabinets, but may not help with sales which is needed to increase revenue. Depending on the economics of hiring more back office and sales this may work for a while. A more difficult decision would be to hire another cabinet maker. You worry about the quality of work. But eventually if you want to exponentially grow your business you must get comfortable with delegating most all of the activities even if you continue to do some of them yourself. You will need to accept the cabinet making quality of the best people you can hire. You must first assess your skills and see where your time would be more beneficial to the company. What jobs can be delegated with the best economic impact? But let this be a fair warning. Once you make the necessary change in your thinking about delegating never lose touch with the customer and quality of your work.

Delegating is an important activity in large corporations as well. However, the biggest failure in corporations are having too many people. More specifically too many people managing managers. I was part of the largest international bank in the world in the 80's. There were 1600 corporations under the corporate umbrella. Many of them actually competed in the same business arenas. I ran a division that had two other corporate entities of my company competing with the same customers. How wasteful and how confusing to the customer. When I joined this monstrous institution, I assumed they were a coordinated, customer focused company. I assumed decisions were made by well-informed managers that were close to the customer. How naïve of me. What I found was a business with layer upon layer of management, even at the local level. There were four and five layers of management away from the customer. This too often resulted in senior managers making large decisions without the understanding of the effect on the street level employees and the customer. I called them "dumb decisions". This was very frustrating. When you have all of these layers of management and so many people managing managers too many people are not looking out for the best interests of the employees/customers but spend all their time preserving their job or feathering their nests (see Congress). Corporate/office politics get in the way of thoughtful business decisions. After ten years watching this and feeling the angst of low information decision making, I vowed never to be part of anything like that again. I spent the rest of my career creating and maintaining the flattest organizations possible. Even when I was atop a $3 billion national sales organization with 125 people, I was never more than two levels away from the street. Flat organizations are totally informed, nimble, flexible and customer focused. Just to illustrate my point, understand that even though I had a Regional manager and local sales managers in every market, I, in combination with the managers interviewed every sales person and physically rode with each of them in their first month with us. This helped me evaluate them beyond just the numbers as well as staring my customers in the eye on a regular basis. In addition to layering, you must avoid allowing too wide of a span of responsibility for each manager. I believe that nobody should have more than 10 direct reports. Trying to effectively managing more than that deteriorates the quality of management. When a manager was at more than ten reports, I began looking for another manager.

In summary, whether there are too few or too many people in an organization, problems result and can upend an otherwise good business plan.

Module 9- Working Environment
Lesson 9-2- Cancer in the Organization

The organization with the most talented, committed and best leaders will fail every time if they allow a cancer to exist in their team. Regardless of the rationalization as to the importance of the individual, retaining this person or group of people will ultimately lead to disaster.

To better understand this statement, we should define what the term means. A cancer in an organization is someone or group of individuals with objectives and goals that are self-serving. These objectives/goals take precedence in their decision making over and above what is best for the team or company. An example is a person who so wants to advance that they would sabotage the efforts of a teammate trying to make the organization succeed. Another is a person with a personal grudge against an individual and devises schemes to discredit them or otherwise injure their standing in the organization. Some cancers are obvious in their tactics and soon will alienate themselves in a healthy organization. Many, however, are more secretive and less conspicuous. They do their work often under the guise of what they express as best for the organization. The antithesis of this is someone who makes decisions with a pure heart. They work for the better of the organization absent of personal gain.

Often times you hear the term "office politics" This is simply an environment of cancer left unchecked and affecting many people on the team. This is the fault of each member of management. "It is not what you know, but who you know" is a comment we have all heard. Often times these are statements of under achieving individuals who want to blame someone else for their lack of success. However, it is sometimes real cancer and must be addressed with open and honest discussion with all members of the team.

Cancer in an organization creates two of the most common symptoms in failed organizations. These are distrust and divisiveness.

Distrust creates an environment whereby more time is spent questioning the motives of an idea or solution by an individual instead of its validity. In other words, the team does not trust that the idea or solution is motivated by a desire to improve or innovate but is borne out of selfish motives. The team spends most of its time determining if this idea or decision is part of a sinister plan. Because time is a limited commodity, often times careful deliberation and sound decision making suffers.

Left unchecked this cancer causes resentment within the team. Sometimes, senior management can be viewed as an accomplice in the plan. Resentment towards the person/group and management grows. Eventually sides are drawn and divisiveness pervades the team and gridlock is a result. Left unchecked this divisiveness leads to people questioning whether they want to be part of an organization like this and they plan to move on.

The best way to avoid this outcome is first to vet new hires by talking to past colleagues and determine their character as displayed at previous positions. Unless a major enlightenment occurs, people do not generally change their ways and will repeat patterns on their new job. Senior management must then communicate and demonstrate their lack of tolerance for bad players. They must make their own decisions "with a pure heart". They should never have private meetings with individuals to plot against another. They must be true to this virtue. Indeed, if the cancer is the senior manager, failure is guaranteed as there is nobody for the team to go to try to correct this behavior. Once a team member is believed to be acting in this manner, the team members should address this privately with the individual. This gives them the opportunity to clarify and defend their actions. If they still feel this person/group is acting in this manner they should meet with senior management. Senior management must treat this as any other conflict and rectify the situation. They must not sweep this under the rug or ignore hoping it will go away. It will not and will eventually cripple the organization. They must always reiterate the no tolerance policy on this subject.

If the person believes they are under scrutiny and truly are guilty, they usually move on as they know they will not get away with it any longer.

Module 9- Working Environment
Lesson 9-3- Meetings- useful but not a social hour

Communications within an organization are the lifeblood of its existence. A lack of communications can lead to its failure. When people are unaware of what the business plans are, the goals, expectations, growth plan and ultimate plan for the future, everything is left to a lack of trust, no sense of inclusion, mistrust and unfounded speculation. Organizations must communicate often to achieve their goals and keep their people.

On the other hand, a group can over-communicate. And worse have meetings with no clear understanding as to why they are meeting or what they want to accomplish. I have seen this first hand. Most of the time it occurs in staff teams as opposed to line/sales groups. In the case of the latter, the nature of their jobs dictates a strict time management approach to their work. Often being commissioned, they will not stand for time spent not forwarding their objectives. Even their management understands this approach and are very sensitive to their impatience with wasting their time. That is why planning a sales meeting is so challenging. There must be a real benefit to the participants and the meeting must be crisp. If you are in a sales meeting and you see the folks looking at their watches you should know that either the content is weak, the benefit is unclear or it's just taking too long.

When it comes to staff folks, the challenges are a bit different even within the groups. The line staff, the ones really doing the day to day work, think more like sales people and do not want to waste their time. They are generally not as impatient as sales, but nonetheless must see the benefit of the meeting.

That leaves the staff managers. Often the problem is not their impatience but a tendency to spend too much time in meetings. It is easy to fall into the habit of going from meeting to meeting and not really getting things done. It is the role of a leader to make sure the time and money of an organization is well spent. Certainly, the advent of video conferencing and other communications methods are helpful. But the structure and efficiency of a well-planned, crisp and effective meeting is always required. Instilling the proper work ethic includes time and meeting management. There are many books on these subjects and I urge you to read at least one on each of them. I attended several courses on each and benefited from the understanding. Here are just a couple thoughts I will share, but research more on your own.

- First step is to try and find a good reason not to have the meeting. Is there another way to accomplish the same thing without dragging everyone into a room or a virtual room?
- Make sure you know what you must accomplish and have an idea of the result of the meeting is expected. A clear plan that is crisply executed will improve your chances of success.
- Before the meeting make sure you communicate with the meeting attendees the timing, reason and goals for the meeting. Often you can have them prepare some pre-work to bring to the meeting to facilitate the event.
- During the meeting stay on point and do not allow the conversations to drift into areas not in the agenda. You can keep a list of these other items and later try to address them if time permits or find another time or way to address them.
- Starting and ending times for meetings must be established and you must strictly adhere to them. The meeting should start promptly and do not wait for late arrivals. They may miss something that time but everyone will be on time in the future when they know of your commitment to everyone's time. I used to publish the start time at two minutes before the hour or half hour. (Meeting starts at 9:58 AM) This gets everyone's attention and makes your point.
- Do not make it too comfortable. Food and coffee provided for meetings not scheduled over lunch gives the impression of a leisure activity. For shorter meetings I actually removed the chairs from the room. It is amazing how quick you get to the point when you are standing versus leisurely sitting with your feet up. Even for brief meetings in my office, I would stand as they came in and not invite them to sit. In and out 5 minutes tops.

People appreciate when you value their time so much as to take the steps to insure a clean crisp and successful meeting. Take the time to make the time well spent.

Final Thoughts

I started writing this book about ten years ago right after the real estate crash that imploded the industry, I was in. I thought I had experienced enough in my then thirty-year career to fill a book. I wrote the outline first. What subsequently transpired taught me that my business career was not only not over, but I was able to learn and see enough in the ten years that followed to add over 30% to the final content of this book. You never stop learning. You also learn far more from difficult times. The post 2008 world was much more than difficult. It resulted in a quantum leap in my thinking and my metamorphosis as a business person. The business world I lived in literally disappeared overnight. All this at the age of 56. *Spoiler alert, "Age matters when you are looking for a job"*. It also taught me the tenuous nature of success and corporate stature. I went from a senior executive of a national firm earning significant income to an older guy looking to find a job in a business sector that was still shrinking and either in a downsizing or bankruptcy mode. It was during this time that I most benefited from 1) a disciplined personal financial strategy and, 2) a mindset of not ever forgetting my roots and not buying into the elevated status to which some people placed me.

1) My personal financial strategy was simple. I never lived or financially committed myself to a level that ever even approached my higher income levels. This means, once I began to earn significantly higher income, I never even lived at my means let alone above my means. We certainly enjoyed the additional money and did some wonderful travel, paid for some nice weddings and did smell the roses along the way, but never materially changed my expenses. We already had a beautiful home, had nice cars but during the good years we could have afforded much more house. We could have had much more expensive cars, boats, etc. But we chose to put away as much money as we could. I knew that one day the top pay would change and never wanted to have financial commitments that I could not afford at half my income. I benefited from an amazing wife who always kept me grounded and saved money like a machine and always found deals at the stores. God bless Maryellen, for without her we could not have retired in the manner we did. I was constantly preaching to my people at work about following a conservative strategy. Many of my folks were earning $500,000 and $600,000 per year. Some listened others did not and suffered after 2008.

2) I never forgot where I came from. I knew I was still that kid from the other side of Hollywood, Fl that did not have much in the beginning. I never felt entitled to success or fortune. I appreciated everything that I earned and every kindness afforded me and opportunity anyone ever gave me. I always did much of my own written communications and always stayed close to the people. I knew and watched the people doing the heavy lifting every day. I generally knew what they did. So, when everything hit the fan, I had the knowledge and skills to do whatever was required to make a living. I also had the humility to do whatever job I needed to take care of my family. No job was ever beneath me. Thanks Mom and Dad.

Finally, I want to thank my wonderful family and friends who supported and loved me unconditionally. To two special ladies without whom my success would never have been achieved, Debbie and Karen. These two ladies were with me for many years. They worked so hard, were so good at what they did, cared about me so much and kept me from screwing up more times than I will ever know. Love you guys. To my wonderful kids, Nicole and Chris, you have both made me proud and inspire me. To their special spouses, Dave and Katie, love you forever. To my grandchildren, well, I could go on forever but I only wish and pray for your health, happiness and safety throughout your lives. To my dear, dear wife Maryellen who put up with me, supported me, raised terrific children and saved our money. I love and thank you and I am a better person for being married to the best person I know. I certainly married up.

In conclusion, my hope is that you can glean at least one piece of information that will help you succeed in life. If so, my career may have a lasting impact on others. I attribute whatever success I have had to the wonderful people with which I have had the pleasure to have been associated. They made me look good and brought much joy and satisfaction to my life. God Bless you.

Recommended Reading

Seven Habits of Highly Effective People by Steven R. Covey

Swim with the Sharks Without Being Eaten Alive by Harvey Mackay

Raving Fans: A Revolutionary Approach to Customer Service by Kenneth H. Blanchard, Sheldon Bowles, Foreword by Harvey MacKay

Spin Selling by Neil Rackham

In Search of Excellence by Tom Peters

www.ingramcontent.com/pod-product-compliance
Lightning Source LLC
Chambersburg PA
CBHW070425180526
45158CB00017B/760